The Gulf Coast

For Susan

Copyright © 1984 by C. C. Lockwood
All rights reserved
Designer: Joanna Hill
Typeface: Linotron Bembo
Typesetter: Moran Colorgraphic
Printer and binder: Toppan Printing Company, Tokyo, Japan

LIBRARY OF CONGRESS CATALOGING IN PUBLICATION DATA

Lockwood, C. C., 1949–
    The Gulf Coast.

    Includes index.
    1. Natural history—Gulf Coast (U.S.) 2. Gulf Coast (U.S.)—De-
scription and travel.   I. Title.
QH104.5.G84L63   1984   508.76   83-25614
ISBN 0-8071-1170-8

Contents

Acknowledgments

The author would like to express thanks to the hundreds of people who have helped this book come to pass. He must also excuse himself for those he may forget to include, but they are just as important as those listed here.

Many thanks to Susan Waters, whose suggestions on the words and pictures were invaluable in the early stages of this book, and to the publisher, Louisiana State University Press, especially my editor Martha Hall, designer Joanna Hill, Les Phillabaum, Beverly Jarrett, and John Easterly. *National Geographic* magazine deserves special thanks, for some of the photographs included herein were done while shooting the Mississippi Delta story published in their August 1983 issue.

Some of the many others who helped by giving me information or taking me to their special places along the Gulf Coast are: Rita Arnold, Hugh Bateman, Bonnie Bell, Walter Berry, Wayne Bettoney, Captain Brownie Brown, Gary Burke, Robert H. Charbreck, Phil Cohagen, Ed Collinsworth, Carol Cordes, John Day, Alan Ensiminger, Doris Falkenheiner, John Fitzsimons, Ted B. Ford, Charles Fryling, Robert Gay, Red Giddens, Bill Grabill, Roger Greene, Richard W. Gregory, Don Hankla, Robert Helm, Sam Henson, Joe Herring, Ted Heuer, Mark Holloman, Ollie Houck, Sam Jojola, Ted Joanen, Edwin A. Joyce, Jr., Donald Kosin, Randy Lanctot, Thomas M. Leahy, Doug Lee, Joel Lindsey, Archie Lowrey, Thomas D. McIlwain, Irving A. Mendelssohn, Bob Misso, Robert Neuman, John O'Neill, Max Pace, Shea Peyland, Joan Phillips, Gene Rizzo, Laurence Rouse, Jack and Anne Rudloe, Gary E. Saul, Ken Schwindt, Keith Sliman, Chuck Smith, James S. Smith, J. Ernest Snell, Marty Stouffer, Hugh Swingle, Mike Tewes, Eugene Turner, Jake Valentine, William Walker, John Wells, Rusty Wharton, Joe White, Kermit Wurzlow, and Bob Ziobro. Also the following government agencies and organizations lent a hand: Louisiana's Department of Wildlife and Fisheries, the United States Fish and Wildlife Service, the United States National Park Service, the tourist bureaus and state parks personnel of all five states, the Baton Rouge Audubon Society, and the Nature Conservancy.

The Gulf Coast

Introduction

Writing about the coast is tough, for my memory keeps drifting back to places where I would still like to be, such as Horn Island, Mississippi, where I watched cottontail rabbits run from bush to bush among the sand dunes in the silver glow of a full moon. Peaceful days, exciting events, and learning experiences enriched my travels along the Gulf Coast, forging images that were more easily captured in my mind and with my camera than on paper.

In more than thirty years of observing the great outdoors, I have noticed repeatedly how wildlife and the environment work together and how man tries to fit into it. At no place is this more evident than on the coast of the Gulf of Mexico.

I have divided this book according to the five habitats found along the coast. They include: the fringe, its swamps, rivers, and the springs that bring fresh water to the marsh; the marsh, with its four classifications, depending on the salinity; the bays, partially enclosed bodies of water usually surrounded by marsh; the islands, our barriers against storms; and the deep blue, the end as well as the beginning of this chain.

These five interlocking habitats work together like veteran baseball players to form the Gulf Coast ecosystem. Just as a ball team can't play without its first baseman, the coast could not function without one of its parts.

I have learned the basics of how this system works, and I hope I have explained it interestingly and simply throughout the five chapters.

Each habitat depends on the others, and man depends on the whole coastal ecosystem. Things have changed since J. W. Collins, master of the *Albatross*, wrote these comments in 1885 following an extensive fisheries survey in the Gulf of Mexico.

But while we may reasonably assume that the fisheries of the Gulf may attain much greater proportion than they now have, it is not probable that they will ever reach an importance at all comparable with such fisheries as those of New England, simply because there are not the enormous resources to draw from for a large supply

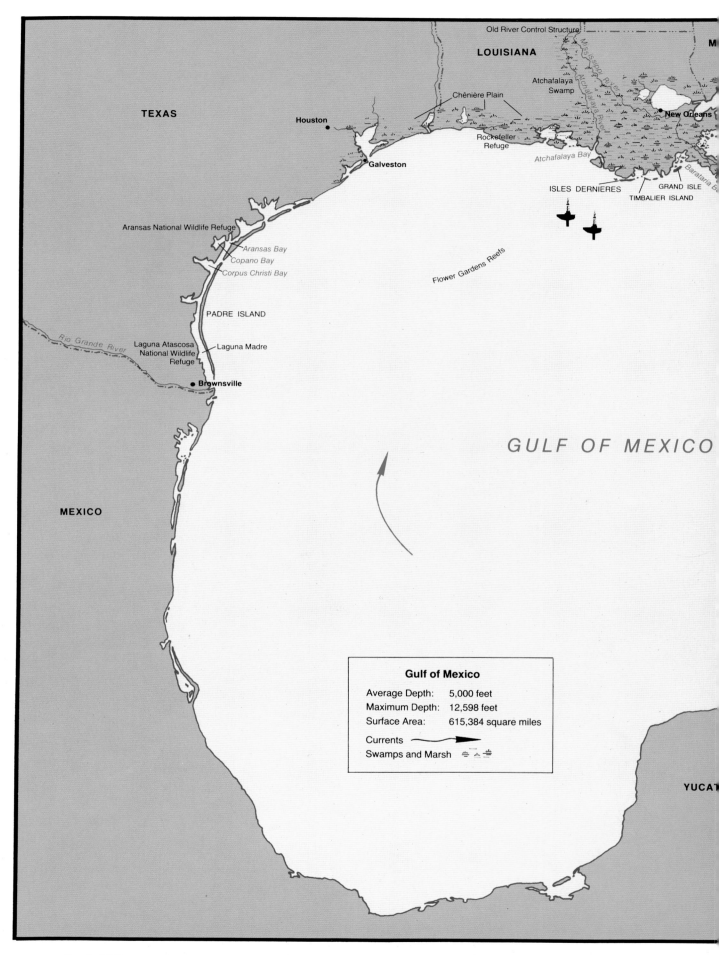

MAP 1 The Gulf Coast

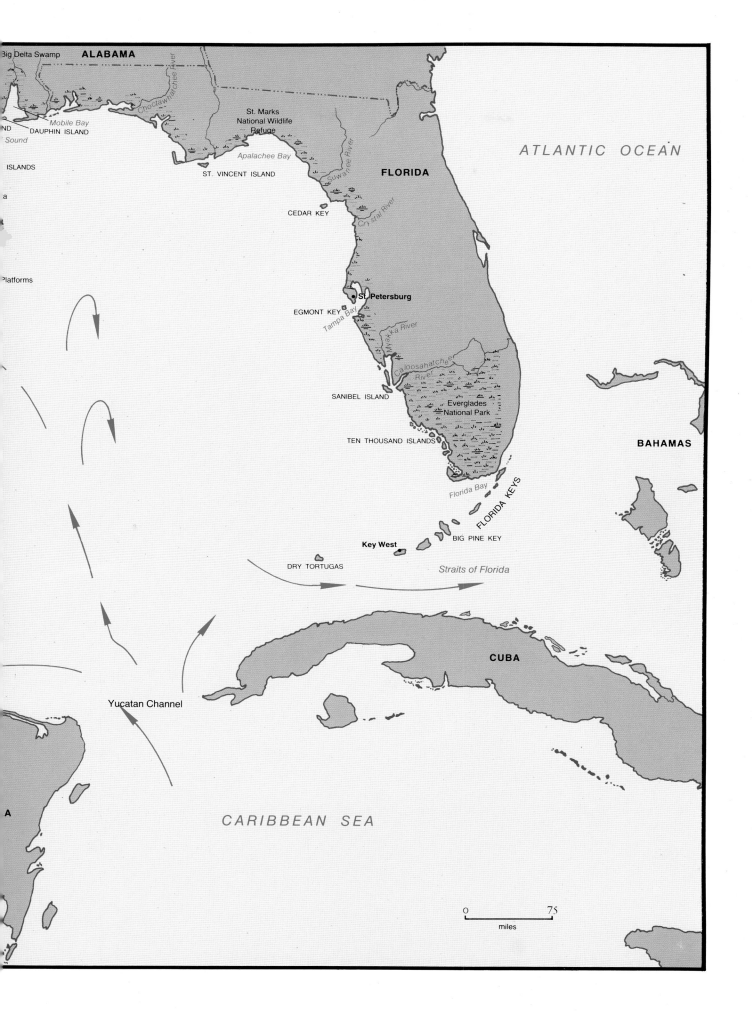

ALABAMA

Big Delta Swamp

Mobile Bay

DAUPHIN ISLAND

Sound

ISLANDS

Platforms

St. Marks
National Wildlife
Refuge

Choctawhatchee River

Apalachee Bay

ST. VINCENT ISLAND

FLORIDA

Suwannee River

CEDAR KEY

Crystal River

ATLANTIC OCEAN

St. Petersburg

EGMONT KEY

Tampa Bay

Myakka River

Caloosahatchee River

SANIBEL ISLAND

Everglades
National Park

TEN THOUSAND ISLANDS

BAHAMAS

Florida Bay

FLORIDA KEYS

Key West

BIG PINE KEY

DRY TORTUGAS

Straits of Florida

Yucatan Channel

CUBA

CARIBBEAN SEA

A

0   75
miles

Labels on image: FRINGE, Swamp, Fresh Marsh, Bald Cypress, Submerged, Bayou, Salt Marsh

MAP 2 The Five Habitats of the Gulf Coast

of material, and also because these southern species are not likely to fill so important a place in cured food as do the staple production of northern seas.

How wrong he was. We have learned how valuable the Gulf Coast is. Commercial landings in the Gulf grew from an insignificant level in 1885 to 6 percent of the U.S. total in 1940, to 12 percent in 1950, to 26 percent in 1960, and to 35 percent in 1970—a fishery worth half a billion dollars.

Our expanding coastal population, which had a 27 percent increase compared to the U.S. average of 11 percent from 1970 to 1980, needs the natural resources as well as the man-made industries of outdoor recreation, tourism, boatbuilding, shipping, oil ex-

ploration, and the associated services that provide for and care for all the people involved.

What would happen if we lost one of those interlocking habitats? It could happen. In the 1920s there was a resort and gambling casino on the Isle of Capri, a small island near Horn Island, Mississippi. A Chicago florist bought all of the island's sea oats to make floral arrangements. Virtually the entire crop of sea oats, which held the sand dunes together, were harvested. With nothing left to anchor the dunes a 1926 hurricane washed most of the sand away. The island no longer exists.

Let's suppose we lost all of our barrier islands. Not only would we lose a great recreational resource, but now the waves of the Gulf would roll directly into the

BAY   BARRIER ISLAND   DEEP BLUE

GULF OF MEXICO

Scrub Live Oak

Sandbar

Submerged Grass

Sea Oats

Dunes

Salt Marsh   Slash Pine

marsh and eventually erode it. Since 90 percent of our commercially caught fish breed or spend some part of their life cycle in the marsh, we would lose the greater part of our commercial fishery.

A chain reaction would begin. The seafood restaurants, tourism, boatbuilding would slow. Without the draw of fishing and beaches an exodus would begin. Without islands and marsh to stop the storms' siege, hurricanes would pose a greater threat to our coastal cities. Fearful people would move, and soon the Gulf Coast would become the Ghost Coast.

An unlikely scenario, maybe, but man has proved he can do about anything.

Fortunately, the system is still working, and we haul in one-third of the United States' commercial

catch of fish and shellfish. The question is whether we can maintain it.

Perhaps this book will help the reader learn something of value about the beauties and bounties of the Gulf Coast. If we understand and appreciate how our environment works, perhaps we can live constructively within it rather than fight against it.

1 The Fringe

The fringe along the Gulf of Mexico has varied beginnings.

Its salty sand flats, dry and dusty, covered with yucca and mesquite, begin in southwest Texas. Eastward the coastline changes into a stately kingdom of bald cypress and tupelo that cast their reflections in tannin-colored swamp water that extends as far as 120 miles into Louisiana. Pine-covered hilly peninsulas jut between the swamps into the marsh. The great diversity in Florida's pinelands, cabbage palm hammocks, and crystal clear springs border the Gulf on to its easternmost reaches.

Exploring freshwater springs was the high point of my travels in Florida. I never dreamed water could be so clear. There are seventy-eight major springs in the continental United States; Florida's twenty-seven pump out eight billion gallons of sparkling clean water every day. Because it is filtered through the many miles of porous limestone known as the Florida aquifer, this water, ranging from sixty-seven to seventy-three degrees Fahrenheit, is pure and free of pesticides, herbicides, and metals.

I stopped first at Wakulla Springs, a private wildlife refuge resort where I found Florida's deepest springs. Divers have followed it to a depth of 250 feet.

Our jungle tour boat glided close by a limpkin, its slender downcurved bill excavating apple snails from their shells. Great blue herons, nesting ospreys, bald eagles, and white ibis watched us from the trees. A gathering of coots, gallinules, and American widgeons parted to let us pass, and in the clear water around us, turtles and alligators swam with bass, catfish, and spotted gar.

Most of Florida's springs are on its west coast, all in areas populated by a similar variety of wildlife, but none so concentrated or tame as that at Wakulla's refuge.

The springs usually become short rivers that blend with salt water as they near the Gulf. These estuarine environments provide breeding grounds or a warm winter haven for such marine creatures as the manatee. A warm-blooded mammal also known as the sea cow, the manatee cannot survive the Gulf's winter temperatures of 55 to 65 degrees, so it comes to Crys-

A great egret guards its fuzzy three-week-old chicks in their nest in the Atchafalaya Basin (left).

tal River and the perpetual 72-degree waters.

Finding the manatees is easiest on the coldest days of February, and I picked a dilly. At 7:30 A.M. the temperature was 39 degrees when I met Charles Talley at the pier on Crystal River to photograph the manatees. Talley, an outspoken manatee lover, is the owner of a fleet of dilapidated marine craft.

He greeted me, "Great day for manatees. Cold, clear, and no wind. We'll see them."

As we pulled out of the cove, a raft of coots ran, webbed feet pattering, across the surface of the shallow water before taking off. In a patch of white fog a pair of canvasbacks bobbed underwater for breakfast as brown pelicans and terns dived through the air. Watching them plunge into the water, I shivered, knowing I would soon be swimming, too. I was beginning to wonder if our small thermos of hot chocolate would be enough.

The leaky skiff lumbered along slowly, pushed by an antique 25-horsepower engine. But we were in no hurry, and propeller blades are the manatee's worst enemy.

Areas of Crystal River and King's Bay are manatee sanctuaries with signs posted by the Florida Marine

Black waters from the Myakka River surround live oaks during a season of unusually high water.

A manatee cow and her calf enjoying the warm waters of the spring-fed Crystal River

Patrol reading, MANATEE AREA—IDLE SPEED. Rounding Banana Island, now owned and protected by Nature Conservancy, we anchored near the main spring. "Manatees," Talley yelled. And I began to see bristly nostrils poke through the glassy surface. Shivering but eager to get into the water, I shed my clothes and pulled on my wetsuit.

I slid quietly over the gunnel and entered the clear and warmer aquatic world. Almost immediately through the hydrilla waving in the current came two manatees, a mother and calf. Excitedly, I adjusted the exposure of my Nikonos. The mother was at least twelve feet long. Swimming close by her side was her calf, its wrinkled knobby skin a few sizes too large. Coming straight at me, albeit very slowly, they looked like two fat torpedoes. What a sight! Finally, when they reached perfect position just three feet away, I snapped the shutter. The tiniest ripples on the surface reflected in a patchwork pattern on their rounded backs while the white sandy bottom lit up their bellies.

Now they would leave. The logical expectation was that having got my lucky shot I would see the subjects swim off and I'd have to wait a long time to ever see another one that close. But to my intense pleasure, for the next three hours I swam and played with eleven manatees. One was dragging a floating radio transmitter and another was so fat in pregnancy that I thought she might calve before my camera.

As I slowly surfaced I could hear Talley yelling at the boaters now crowded near us, "Slow, there's a manatee under your boat. . . . You're going to chop them up with your propeller!" For sixteen years, Talley has been teaching diving and taking people to see the manatees. In addition to bearing propeller scars from careless boaters, these endangered mammals, Talley claims, suffer miscarriages caused by herbicides used to kill hydrilla. An exotic plant brought to the United States by pet store suppliers to decorate aquariums, hydrilla now grows wild and blocks Florida waterways, much like the imported water hyacinth in Louisiana.

Later that day Talley took us to the Rainbow River, which is known to have the clearest Florida springs. I believe it, for upon entering the crystal water, I felt as if I were flying until I saw a red-eared turtle swim by. I saw rainbow reflections on the sandy bottom as sunlight passed through prisms of the water's rippling surface. Bass, bluegill, and eels glided by as the red and green ruffled arms of watercress swayed in the current. On the way back, we spotted a four-foot alli-

The predominant tree of Gulf Coast swamps, the bald cypress lines

Lichen on a live oak bark near the Myakka River

the Choctawhatchee River, Florida.

The snowy egret, one of the four species of Gulf Coast egrets, is identified by its golden feet (below).

12 *Known as the clearest of Florida's twenty-seven major springs, the Rainbow River shows off its aquatic plants.*

Once seriously endangered, the American alligator has made a strong comeback in Louisiana and Florida.

Unlike a parasite, the resurrection fern, an epiphyte, does not harm its host tree.

On a cypress knee, an anhinga dries its wings after an underwater swim in search of fish.

gator near the shore, and I dived in with my snorkle just in time to get a blurred picture of its tail as the creature swam into a bankside den.

Elsewhere in Florida I visited live oak and cabbage palm hammocks draped with aerial orchids, spanish moss, and other epiphytes. *Picturesque* is an understatement for the tropical magnificence of Florida's coastal fringe.

Protected by the world's longest chain of barrier islands, the south Texas coast is as tropical as Florida's, but the difference between the two is immeasurable. This part of Texas gets less than 20 percent of the rainfall that Florida gets, making it a near desert. A hundred years ago it was endless brush country, covered with impenetrable tangles of mesquite, prickly-pear cactus, ebony trees, catclaw, and spanish dagger. These plants bristle with weapons that make the terrain inhospitable to all but the hardiest humans. Fertilized each year by the overflowing Rio Grande River, the bountiful land was once rich in North American as well as tropical wildlife. The soil and climate, however, were perfect for farming, so the farmers came.

Now, after a century of land clearing by methods such as chaining, less than 1 percent of the brush

Yucca, a barbed plant species of the Laguna Atascosa refuge

Seeds caught in the crotch of a dying tree gave life to a prickly-pear cactus (far left).

Where land meets sea, a young spike buck stands alert between nibbles of marsh grass.

Turkey gobblers, Aransas National Wildlife Refuge, Texas

country remains. Terrifyingly efficient, chaining employs two bulldozers dragging a chain between them that quickly rips down every plant in its path. The remaining stubble is then burned, and the area converted to farmland.

The Rio Grande has been leveed to contain rising water after heavy rains, so the land can no longer drink the overflow and be replenished with valuable nutrients each spring. When bugs threatened cropland, massive amounts of pesticides were applied, toxifying the water in south Texas. Mexican farmers still use heavy doses of DDT, banned in the United States, even though such insects as the tobacco budworm have become immune to the deadly hydrocarbon poison.

Patches of brush do still exist. At Laguna Atascosa National Wildlife Refuge eight thousand acres of brush serve as prime (and in America possibly the last remaining) habitat for the ocelot. Slightly larger than a house cat and rarely seen by man, this secretive feline can scoot like greased lightning through brush that would take a man two days to get through with a bulldozer.

I had the opportunity to run a trapline with Mike Tewes, a University of Idaho graduate student who is making a study of the ocelots of south Texas. Most of

From a thorny perch a mockingbird views the south Texas sunset.

his work has been on the refuge, where he estimates a population of thirty-five ocelots. One of those was in the second trap we checked, a juvenile male with a radio collar that Mike had attached four months earlier. Mike sedated the young cat, then weighed, measured, photographed, and picked a few ticks off before putting him back in the cage.

Late that evening, I got the chance to see the cat in action when Mike opened the trap. The animal took a second to gather his thoughts, then bolted so fast that my 1/1000-of-a-second shutter speed caught only a blur.

Originally, the refuge was created to provide a winter home for America's largest group of redhead ducks. Tens of thousands of crimson heads bob in the rippling water of Laguna Madre. In addition, the refuge offers habitat to 313 other bird species, making it a favorite stop for roving bird watchers.

While wandering through the bushes looking for the iridescent green jays, I spotted a roadrunner dancing through the underbrush with a lizard dangling from its long beak. Along with the green jay, I added the chachalaca, pauraque, olive sparrow, and long-billed thrasher to my life bird list while at Laguna.

About two hundred miles to the north I stopped at Aransas National Wildlife Refuge, winter home of the

Nature's dry cleaner, the sun, helps some turkey vultures remove parasites from their wings.

A crepuscular creature, this white-tailed buck begins feeding at sunset (right).

most well-known endangered species, the whooping
crane. In the 1930s there were only fourteen whoop-
ers. Today seventy-three use Aransas each year and at
least thirty more are divided among a western flock,
zoos, and the Patuxent Wildlife Research Center re-
covery program in Maryland.

In one afternoon I got to see thirty-six of the Aransas flock from Captain Brownie Brown's gaudy pink
sight-seeing boat, the *Whooping Crane*. Bald-headed
Brownie has probably shown more people an endangered species than anyone else in the world. Up to
150 birders line the top of his double-decked craft and
listen to the salty old captain recite his guarantee.
"You get your full refund if we don't see the whoop-
ers up close." He'll brag on his coffee (he claims it
cures seasickness) and even offer some important information, like how the cranes recently have been discovered in the fringe eating acorns under the live
oaks.

The oaks here are a dwarf or scrub variety that
bends to the north from the sculpturing action of constant sea breezes. At dawn I saw sixty-three vultures
perched in an oak thicket with wings outstretched in
the faint sun, demonstrating nature's method of dry
cleaning. Below them was a white-tailed buck with

A recent migrant from Mexico, the armadillo   *White-tailed doe* (below)

Eastern meadowlark, Rockport, Texas

one antler and a red spot where the other had just
fallen off.

Seeing wildlife is what Aransas is all about. If you
don't see deer, turkey, and armadillo on the loop tour
road, you're not looking very hard.

Aransas, all of Texas, in fact the whole Gulf Coast
is good for seeing wildlife, especially birds. Texas
leads the nation with 546 birds on its state list. Louisiana and Florida are in the top ten with more than 400
species each. One reason is the migration, that yearly
phenomenon that sends two-ounce birds with six-
inch wings on thousand-mile journeys—south in the
fall and north in the spring. Since all of these birds
have to cross the Gulf en route to South America, it's
not surprising that the coastal states attract huge numbers.

The Chenier plain is one of the country's birding
hot spots. Stretching two hundred miles from East
Bay, Texas, to Vermilion Bay, Louisiana, is a unique
habitat that has formed from Mississippi River silt
over five thousand years. Oak-covered ridges ten to
fifty miles long run parallel with the coast, creating islands of trees in the marsh—motels for migrating
birds.

Fallout is an event that usually happens only on
nasty spring days when a strong north wind is blow-

ing wet and cold, perfect weather for staying by the television set. But if you'll get yourself out to High Island, Texas, or Johnson Bayou, Louisiana, you'll see birds galore.

I did. It was a drizzling cold mid-April day when I went to the small Louisiana chenier known as Peveto Beach Woods. Upon entering the woods I could hear only the raucous voices of gulls on the beach a quarter of a mile away. At 11 A.M. I climbed into a mulberry tree and wondered if what I had heard about bird fall-out was true.

In his book, *The Birds of Louisiana*, Dr. George Lowery says that birds migrating with a south wind (tail wind) won't land until they are far inland; but those bucking a north wind on their long journey from Yucatan stop at the first available tree, the cheniers.

A little past noon the quiet was over. Whistles, peeps, and cheeps of every tone rang out from birds of every color. My tree was beginning to look like a page of paint samples: red and black of the scarlet tanager; rose, white and black of the rose-breasted grosbeak; blue, red, yellow-green, and purple of the painted bunting; and the brilliant golden yellow of the prothonotary warbler.

Wood duck, a colorful, shy resident of Gulf Coast swamps

A catbird, one of the many spring migrants to cross the Texas-Louisiana coast

A viceroy butterfly feeds on the exotic water hyacinth.

On its spring migration across the Gulf, a scarlet tanager rests on a tree on the Louisiana chenier.

Belly down on a thick branch, the warbler let its wings hang in exhaustion. With open beak and dangling tongue, it looked as if it were panting. Before I climbed down, four more species settled into my tree.

In the next hour, I counted twenty-three species, and I probably missed a few others since I am not an expert. In a full day, a good birder will see many more. Several years ago, Bruce Crider and Paul McKenzie counted 183 species during the spring migration. I'm not that dedicated, but seeing a brilliant scarlet tanager full frame in my viewfinder was a great treat.

The fall migration provides equally good birding, but without the fallout or the color spectrum. The warblers, for instance, lose their colorful breeding plumage in autumn, making identification more difficult for the amateur. Easier to recognize are the great flocks of wintering ducks and geese. Drawing about 64,000 hunters each year, the cheniers and surrounding area are the most popular waterfowl grounds in Louisiana.

Forming the cheniers is not all the Mississippi River has done for the Gulf Coast; it is in fact a master marshmaker. Flowing and growing from thirty-one states and two Canadian provinces, its tumultuous

Avian architect, a cattle egret sizes up a stick before adding it to its nest.

flow reached 1.3 billion gallons of muddy water per day during the 1973 flood. For 7,500 years it has been snaking across Louisiana's shallow bays looking for a place to drop its 356,000 metric tons of sediment each day.

Old Man River has provided enough good earth to build 19,000 square miles of coastal Louisiana, an area larger than Rhode Island, Delaware, Connecticut, and Hawaii combined. Reckoning in dollars alone, at $500 per acre, that comes to more than $6 billion worth of land.

This vast rich land was formed by a deltaic process. The river built its way to the Gulf until somewhere, 200 to 300 miles inland, the flow would change to another tributary in search of a shorter route to the Gulf. Through this process, five deltas were made and four were abandoned. Today's delta, the Plaquemine-Modern Delta Complex, is here to stay. At least the United States Army Corps of Engineers says so.

With thousands of miles of levee and the Old River Control Structure blocking the Mississippi from its natural route down the Atchafalaya River, all that valuable sediment has reached the end of the line. The long birdfoot *lobes* of the delta are nearing the continental shelf where the bottom drops hundreds of feet.

A pilot boat meets a ship at Pilottown, Louisiana.

Because of fog and heavy traffic, all ships must have a pilot to travel the Mississippi River.

Now, rich Iowa topsoil disappears over the edge, down to Davy Jones's locker. With very little new silt to nourish them, the swamps and marshes are sinking.

At the growing rate of fifty square miles per year ($16 million worth of land per year, priced at $500 per acre), Louisiana has lost five hundred square miles of land since 1954.

The Mississippi River has indeed given us a lot. Most of the 19,000 square miles still exist in marsh, farms, towns, and swamps. The Atchafalaya Basin, a jewel among swamps, sprawls 120 miles from the Gulf, where it meets the Mississippi as the major distributary, gulping down as much as one-third of the Mississippi's flow during the flood season. The Old River Control Structure at the rivers' junction prevents the Atchafalaya from carrying its natural load of more than half the water and becoming the new Mississippi.

The basin is the epitome of a cooperative ecosystem. As America's largest overflow river basin swamp, it starts amid dense hardwood bottomland in central Louisiana. This higher land supports oak, pecan, sweetgum, and other hardwoods to make prime habitat for deer, turkey, wood duck, and the world's largest wintering population of woodcock.

White ibis at a rookery in the Atchafalaya Basin (overleaf)

Moonrise over an Indian mound near Lafitte, Louisiana

A unique beehive; most are inside hollow trees.

The silt-laden waters then pass into the bald cypress-tupelo swamp to the south, soaking the boles of these flood-hardy trees for most of the year. Safe from predators above the high water, great egrets nest in the green fernlike foliage of the cypress branches in squawking colonies of thousands. The egret and a multitude of other animals share with man the annual harvest of 42 million pounds of crawfish.

Slowing as it spreads, the mighty Atchafalaya flows into the marsh below Morgan City, pushing the salt water out into Atchafalaya Bay. Water levels in the swamp can vary by twenty feet during a flood year or at least eight feet during normal years. Nutrient-rich water supports flora and fauna alike, cleansing itself as it passes through miles of swamp and marsh vegetation.

I spent four years wading and walking, paddling and swimming, wandering and exploring the swampland country the Atakapa Indians named the Atchafalaya (meaning long river). I learned firsthand, unscientifically, how fish and fowl, land and water, plant and animal fit together, with man on the edge trying to squeeze his way in.

Consider the raccoon. Sitting in an oak tree, I watched one search for acorns. With supersensitive hands, he felt for them in the muddy shallow water,

Raccoons are abundant in all habitats of the Gulf Coast.

The Big Muddy, important as a shipping corridor, but more so to bring nutrients to south Louisiana's swamps and marshes

Cattail goes to seed.

the same as he would for crawfish in the cypress-tupelo habitat, or fiddler crabs in the marsh, or oysters in the bay, or mullet on the islands. The raccoon has adapted to all the habitats. The shrimp flourishes in three habitats, the porpoise in two, and the periwinkle in only one.

If nature were a computer, it would have the most valuable program around, for it has been working miracles for millions of years. The swamp in the fringe is one important micro chip.

2 The Marsh

"Marshes are mucky/Icky and yucky." This little rhyme a friend jokingly told me is partially true. In a physical sense, coastal wetlands are an environment hostile to mankind. And no one knows it better than those who work there. An old Cajun fisherman mused, "If I had the tough hide of a 'gator, the webbed feet of a duck, and them big wings of the blue heron, I get around this marsh just fine."

My dreams are similar. If I could soar, I'd be a golden eagle; as a mammal, I'd choose to be a river otter. I decided this long ago because both creatures are so efficient that they have time for recreation. In one of their bodies I could travel the marsh effortlessly. But I'm stuck with my human body, its plantigrade feet with unwebbed toes that quickly sink into the muck, hair-poor skin too soft for the sharp grasses and the prickling beaks of swarming mosquitos, and a hand with an extraordinary opposable thumb that's too slow to catch fish or other live food.

Although man himself will never be able to slither through the cattails like the broad-banded water snake, he has learned to depend on the marshes for an abundant supply of natural resources. Those renewable resources are valued at $50,000 to $80,000 per acre based on the marshes' capability to filter pollutants from the water and produce fish and fur. Add the oil resources (nonrenewable) and recreational opportunities, and the value exceeds that of prime city real estate. Furthermore the marsh produces these values year after year. Yet for quick dollars landowners and developers want to drain and convert marshland.

With all its rich resources, the marsh fails to produce substantial income for the landowner. He doesn't actually profit from the shrimp catch even though the shrimp may use his marsh as nursery grounds. Income from hunting and trapping leases in the marsh is nominal compared to payments from successful oil exploration. Petroleum is a finite resource, so landowners search for a land use with a more stable future.

One solution is impoundment of the marsh to prevent saline tidal intervention. Flushed with fresh water, rice can grow in the corralled marsh. With frequent pumping, the drier areas can serve as cow pas-

ture. Unfortunately, these agricultural conversions threaten a fishery worth half a billion dollars. Some 90 percent of the commercially caught fish spend some time in the marsh during their life cycle.

Shrimp, the most valuable seafood, is a perfect example of the necessary link between the marsh and the Gulf waters. The two major species of shrimp, *Penaeus aztecus* (brown shrimp) and *Penaeus seriferus* (white shrimp), spawn in the deep blue, but grow up in the marsh.

The brown shrimp, for example, spawns from spring to early summer in 150 to 360 feet of water. Each female releases millions of eggs into the currents, where they quickly hatch and blend in with the pasture of the sea, plankton. At this stage, each shrimp is a nauplius, a microscopic dot with one eye and three pairs of appendages, resembling a tick with roots growing from it. The planktonic shrimp molts eleven times, going through nauplius, protozoean, and mysis stages before finally resembling a real shrimp in the larval form.

From January to June the larvae make their way into the marshes, where warm shallow water and the tidally inundated marsh grass will provide protection and food. They share these nursery grounds with the larvae and young of the blue crab, the oyster, and var-

Shrimping, whether in double-rigged trawlers (far left) or small family operations (left), yields a catch (below) treasured in many seafood dishes. Great expanses of marsh (overleaf) are necessary to shrimp as a breeding area.

37

Damaging marsh-buggy tracks, usually left by seismograph crews, take years to heal.

ious fishes. Here they will grow into shrimp of marketable size. Then the lunar cycle, tides, and estuarine temperatures lure them back offshore where they grow to jumbo size and produce millions of eggs.

So many eggs are released that the threat of overfishing is insignificant as long as vegetated estuaries for nursery grounds are secure and abundant. Studies around the world have directly linked shrimp landings to the quality and quantity of adjacent marshes.

The brown shrimp likes saltier marshes, whereas the white moves farther inland. All marshes are not the same; they are classified according to salinity, and perform different functions. Seawater is 36 parts per thousand (ppt) salt. In other words, there are 36 pounds of salt in 1000 pounds of water. Marsh is divided into four general categories: fresh marsh with 0 to 1 ppt, intermediate with 1 to 3 ppt, brackish with 3 to 8 ppt, and saline with 8 to 18 ppt.

Without chemically testing the water, a botanist can estimate salinity by the local plant life. The harsh environment of the saline marsh supports a few species of salt-hardy plants. In fact, oystergrass, *Spartina alteriflora*, covers 62 percent of Louisiana's salt marsh, as if challenging other plants to grow in its territory. It and its close relative, *Spartina patens*, or wiregrass, are considered the most important aspect of the marsh.

Least bittern in roseau cane

Ridges along Bayou Carencro support ancient live oaks (below).

(*Patens* covers 55 percent of the brackish and 34 percent of the intermediate marsh in the state.) They produce 5 to 10 tons of organic matter per acre, as much as or more than the best wheat fields in the country.

Animal life, particularly the invertebrates like mollusks, worms, etc., can also be a signal of the salinity. Larger animals may prefer one habitat but can venture into the connecting life zone or even all of them. Crawfish, furbearers, and alligators tend to stay in the fresh marsh whereas blue crabs and shrimp like saltier zones.

I like them all, but think fresh is the prettiest, due to its variety of flora. I spent one spring in Terrebonne Parish, Louisiana, which has one of the largest fresh marshes in the United States.

My first experience there was with Kermit Wurzlow. Kermit promised to take me out to his lease (a section of land leased for hunting from a larger landholder) to see the giant blue iris in bloom. Our scenic ride out the Falgout Canal, Lake DeCade, and Bayou Carencro was uneventful, with Kermit telling tall tales about the fish he had caught in the many years spent at his camp. Upon docking the big boat we transferred our gear to a fourteen-foot john boat with

Giant blue iris (right)

Marsh raccoons do much more swimming than their woodland cousins.

42

Long legs and its coloring give the black-necked slit its name.

Delicate clouds brighten a winter sunrise over a Louisiana fresh marsh (right).

Swamp rabbit, Rockefeller Refuge, Louisiana

Marshland shrubs such as rattlebox (right) offer the only homesites for tree-nesting birds like the eastern kingbird (above).

Protected marsh waters are important in the life cycle of blue crabs.

a 6-horsepower motor and puttered out into the marsh.

Before long we got off the main canal and entered a series of ponds surrounded by bulltongue, one of the most common fresh marsh plants and an excellent waterfowl food. Here and there was a lone iris, but Kermit said he knew a spot where they were thick, and we found it. The stately purplish-blue iris resembled Air Force sentinels guarding the blooming bulltongue whose white petals surround fuzzy green buttons.

After touring the lease, Kermit left me to enjoy a few days of spring at his camp. My exploration began with a jolt of adrenalin when a garfish lifted the bow of my little bateau completely out of the water. Coming to the surface to breathe, the 6-foot alligator gar (the Louisiana record is 9 feet 8 inches) could have turned my boat over had he hit it just right.

Gars are physostomous, a condition that allows the fish to breathe surface air through his swim bladder. This unique adaptation enables him to live in water with zero oxygen content. Whereas most fish can breathe only oxygen-rich water through their gills, the gar can use either its gills or its swim bladder for breathing.

Along the canal I passed a purple gallinule every

A gathering of ibis and egrets usually means a good fishing hole.

Resting on one leg, a pair of willets soak up some winter sunshine.

few hundred yards, some followed by a string of three to eight chicks. The young gallinules were little puffs of black down, not nearly as elegantly dressed as their mother. Her head and belly are a rich iridescent purplish-blue, accented by olive-green wings and back. Topping it off is a blue bald spot above a red beak tipped with yellow. Supported by yellow legs with long slender feet, this beautiful bird is adept at walking on lily pads in search of aquatic insects. Each gallinule rushed across the floating vegetation and into the marsh as I passed.

Entering a pond, I caught a glimpse of a small alligator swimming beneath my boat as I photographed the petite white flower of the fanwort. The tangly arms of this subaqueous plant are a favorite hiding place for young fish and turtles. Perhaps the 'gator was looking for a meal.

Once an endangered species, the alligator has made a grand comeback along the Gulf Coast. Louisiana's alligator population in twelve coastal parishes has grown from a low of 75,000 in the 1950s to 450,000 today. This repopulation is due in part to the research and hard work of the staff at Rockefeller Refuge, a state wildlife preserve in southwestern Louisiana. Ted Joanen, who headed the research, told me that the

Emerging from a duckweed-covered bayou, an alligator carries hundreds of the tiny plants on its head.

The water hyacinth, a lovely nuisance, thrives in the fresh marsh.

best alligator habitat is intermediate marsh. I saw alligators from Key West, Florida, to Aransas, Texas, but the friendliest by far was in Lake Hatch, Louisiana.

Bayou Annie Miller leads marsh tours into Lake Hatch to see a rookery of roseate spoonbills, white ibis, herons, and egrets, but her star attraction is "Baby." Baby is a four-foot alligator who eats chicken on a stick. Annie floats into the lake calling, "Ba-a-a-a-by, Ba-a-a-a-by." And sure enough, the 'gator comes right up to Annie, delighting her passengers.

I have spent a lot of time at the rookery in Lake Hatch, and I assume the 'gators are there for the same reason I am, to see the birds. I come to look; they come to eat. The alligator waits below a tree for a weak chick or an egg to fall. The islands of button-bush and willow are covered with thousands of nesting birds. At sunset it seems as if someone has let the stopper out of a bathtub of white ibis as they pour from the sky, some single file, some in V formation.

On my last day at Kermit's camp I struggled through thick growths of water hyacinths to visit Lovel Island, an ancient Indian shell mound covered with massive moss-draped live oaks. I flushed a great

Of the four types of marsh, fresh marsh has the greatest diversity of

plant life. Sagitaria lines a pond in Terrebonne Parish.

horned owl as I stepped onto the island and later found his nest with three plump owlets inside, craning their necks to study this intruder.

I was surprised to find an armadillo with two babies on the tiny island. Armadillos are terrestrial creatures, and although a few ridges occur along marsh bayous, she had had to do some swimming to get there. Not known for their aquatic prowess, armadillos reportedly have walked across the bottoms of rivers.

Her two babies puzzled me because armadillos usually bear four young of the same sex. It was unlikely that the great horned owl got them since bobcats, coyotes, foxes, and dogs are the armadillo's only predators.

Anyway, the mother was working diligently to provide a cozy home for her small family. In a slow, mechanical fashion she gathered leaves and moss to line her nest in the underground den. Tucking the material under her, she would arch her back, pinching the leaves between her armored plates for transport. As much as half a bushel of nesting material has been found in excavated armadillo dens.

As I silently watched the mother disappear into the den, the two youngsters ambled past me. Armadillos are nearly blind, living by sound and smell. One

A diet of shellfish gives the roseate spoonbill its color.

Among the mangroves a tricolored heron stalks its prey.

caught a whiff of me and came over for closer inspection. He stood on his hind legs, his tiny paws on my knee, and sniffed. He must have smelled danger because he sprang away at top speed as only an armadillo knows how.

During all this quiet time, the deer flies were eating me alive, so I made a quick dash across the island. To my delight I stopped short of a spider web, but two deer flies didn't. They were immediately pounced upon by the hungry arachnid. I spent the next half hour reducing the deer fly population while feeding a spider friend.

The Everglades, a river of grass, begins just south of Orlando and runs till it dumps its waters into Florida Bay. The jagged sawgrass is nourished by a freshwater river fifty miles wide but only six inches deep. Life here depends on the summer rains; tropical moist weather creates a perfect environment for large populations of insects that are the first link in an intricate food chain. The chain leads eventually to the Florida panther, a rare cat that has been extirpated from the rest of its range along the Gulf Coast.

Another endangered species endemic to the Everglades is the snail kite, a slow-flying hawk that feeds exclusively on the apple snail. With the Fish and

Double-crested cormorant

Nostrils at the tip of its head allow the Florida softshell turtle to breathe without emerging.

American coots parade past elephant ear in the Mississippi Delta fresh marsh.

Wildlife Service biologist, Paul Sikes, I watched a kite drop into the marsh, snatch a snail, and fly up to his favorite perch. Paul, who had been studying the kite for six years, told me that the bird's bill was built to the same specifications as the entrance of the snail's shell, perfectly adapting the raptor to his singular diet. No snails means no kites, and the mollusk is getting harder to find as it battles south Florida's human population for the precious water supply.

This demand is lowering the water table so much that sink holes are commonplace and the soil becomes parched. During the drought of 1981, the earth was so dry that the organic peat soil actually burned in marsh grass fires.

Of course, too much water can be destructive. When excessive rains during the winter–spring of 1983 brought flooding to the Everglades, deer habitat was greatly reduced. To deal with the overcrowding, a controversial special deer season was opened, drawing nationwide attention and concern.

The water level is crucial to the process of nesting bird colonies. Huge flocks of wood storks, ibis, egrets, and herons are left without nesting sites when flooding covers the low trees. In drought years the birds' food supplies are inadequate as fish habitat is re-duced. Without water surrounding the nesting col-

A raft of coots congregate in an early morning fog.

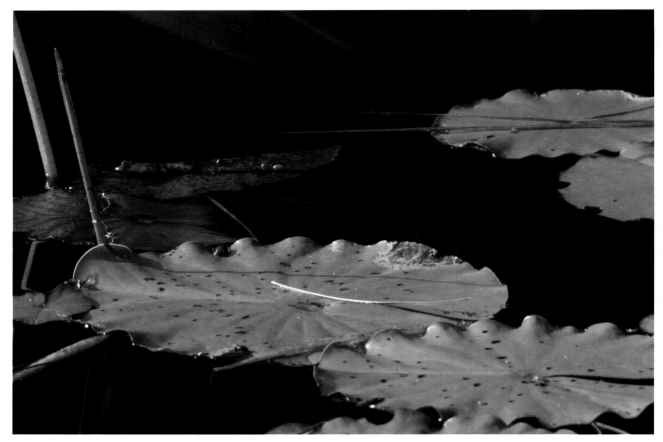

Aquatic vegetation provides food and shelter for marshland animals.

Needlerush marsh at St. Marks National Wildlife Refuge

Salt-marsh pink, Terrebonne Parish marsh

ony, eggs and chicks are subject to predation by land creatures.

Before man took control of water in southern Florida, the Everglades managed its own water level through runoff. Where tidal action brings saltwater to mix with the fresh, a brackish marsh zone exists.

The brackish marsh is a detrital-based community that thrives on decayed matter carried by the constant flush of water. One of the most noticeable detritivores is the fiddler crab. Once while poking around the wiregrass near Mobile Point, I thought I saw a mud flat move. Rubbing my eyes, I took a step, and it moved again like a sheet rippling in the wind. Getting closer, I realized the optical illusion was a pod of at least three thousand fiddler crabs moving in unison. When I got too close, they scattered, running backwards toward their hole-in-the-mud homes.

Fiddlers were named for their one oversized claw that makes them look like they're carrying a fiddle. This pod was grazing on the microscopic detritus (particles of rotting wiregrass) on the mud at low tide.

Another salt-tolerant grass, more properly called a rush, is *Juncus roemerianus* and it prefers the saline marsh. Mississippi's marshes are dominated by this species commonly called needle rush. I decided it was

Like an oasis, cabbage-palm hammocks crop out of Florida's west

Railroad vine, Grand Isle

appropriately named when I hiked through a stand of it and felt the tips poke into my unprotected arms. In the fall the stems of needle rush turn to a greyish tan making a monochromatic scene against the stormy sky.

Endless stands of needle rush are also common along Florida's Gulf coast. Like exotic oases, cabbage palm hammocks crop up sporadically, breaking up the homogeneous landscape. Indians found a variety of uses for the palm. Today the core, or heart, of the tree is a local delicacy in Cedar Key, Florida, where I ordered it in a salad at Johnson's restaurant. The heart-of-palm salad was served topped with a glob of peanut butter sherbet—unique and a little too rich before my meal.

"Marshes are mucky, icky and yucky." Ridiculous! I see vibrant interlocking communities of plant and animal life.

I remember a day in the saline marsh at the mouth of Grand Bayou on Caillou Bay, Louisiana. I was helping Freddie Cox sort shrimp on the deck of his butterfly-net barge. He had caught two full barrels of medium shrimp as the tide rushed back to sea. The shrimp that escaped his nets would someday release their millions of eggs in the deep blue. The less for-

coast salt marsh.

Winter turns the once-green brackish marsh to golden tan (overleaf).

Imported from South America, the nutria is now abundant in the marsh.

61

The anhinga uses its sharp-pointed beak to spear fish.

tunate shrimp were frying up in Freddie's pan.

Three porpoises surfaced in the bay as I walked to the back deck. I watched as the last dollop of sun dropped below the swaying oyster grass. The porpoises leaped completely out of the water to join me as I cheered the setting sun.

3 The Bays

It was my fourth try. Yes, that many times in six weeks I had loaded down my fourteen-foot fiberglass bateau with cameras, blind, tent, food and water, everything carefully wrapped in plastic garbage bags. Each time, I backed down the boat ramp, launched, and ventured out of the Port Mansfield Harbor. Each time, rough seas sent me back to the safety of the harbor. It doesn't take much wind or choppy water to make riding in my craft wet, uncomfortable, and even dangerous, but this was ridiculous. Either I had come at the wrong season or the wind never stops blowing in south Texas.

My bateau was made for the smooth waters of a bayou, not Laguna Madre, a hypersaline bay extending 110 miles from Corpus Christi, Texas, to within a few miles of the Mexican border. Constant southeasterly winds had chopped up the shallow water across the ten-mile width of the bay at Port Mansfield.

This time I was determined to go. My time in south Texas was running out and I wanted to see the bay. Along with the unique aquatic community here, the land cut twenty-five miles up the bay is known for its populations of deer, coyotes, raccoons, and the exotic nilgai antelope. Looking back at tiny Port Mansfield, one of the few towns tucked between the giant ranches owned by the famous Kings and other families, I waterproofed myself for the wet ride. Dressed with hip boots and hooded slicker jacket, I stepped into a garbage bag and taped it around my waist and knees for added protection.

There was nothing I could do to make the trip more comfortable—going fast, slow, tacking—nothing helped. Sheet after sheet of water lashed my face as my bateau pounded against the choppy seas. Salt crystalized on my sunglasses making vision impossible. Removing the glasses was no solution, for my eyes then took the direct punishment. Laguna Madre is extremely salty, sometimes up to 60 ppt, or nearly twice as saline as seawater. Poor circulation from the Gulf is caused by Padre Island, a substantial barrier against seawater intermingling with the bay. Only three tidal passes to the Gulf exist: one near Port Isabel, another at Port Mansfield, and the northern entrance at Port Aransas. Lack of rain and the shallow

A porpoise leads our boat across Aransas Bay.

water contributing to high evaporation also increase the salinity.

If the Laguna were drained, it would take twenty-six months for the Rio Grande and other small streams to fill it back up. The Mississippi River could do the same job in twenty-two hours.

Laguna Madre's ecosystem is not based on detritus and plankton like most of the Gulf of Mexico bays, but rather on benthic plants. Shoal grass is the most abundant plant, but widgeon grass, manatee grass, and turtle grass also carpet the bottom of the bay. Sea grasses thrive in relatively clear and shallow water like that in Laguna Madre. Corpus Christi Bay was once undisturbed like Laguna, but much of its sea grass has now disappeared, the result of turbidity from dredging, constant ship traffic, and industrial runoff.

The value of the sea grasses is most obvious during winter when 78 percent of the world's redhead ducks seek the warm weather and shoal grass in Laguna Madre. Pintail ducks also feed extensively on the grass. Less visible, but equally important, is the aquatic use of the grasses. In addition to various shellfish, five species of finfish feed on the grass. These make up the bulk of the biomass: pinfish, striped mullet, spot, bay anchovy, and tidewater silverside. In

Wind-swept dunes gathered at the edge of sand flats sometimes

flooded by Laguna Madre

Tons of other fish are caught during shrimping in East Bay, Louisiana.

Laguna Madre harbors the largest wintering population of redhead ducks.

Hoping for handouts, a laughing gull follows a shrimp boat in Copano Bay, Texas.

turn these are preyed upon by two popular species of gamefish, the speckled trout and the redfish.

Before the status of the two species was changed from commercial to gamefish, commercial netters hauled out of Laguna Madre 38 percent of the Texas speckled trout catch and 60 percent of the redfish. The redfish spawns in the Gulf and the juveniles move into the seagrass after hatching; the trout feeds and spawns in the same area.

I couldn't see any of this happening down under, as I opted for full speed to get the wet ride over as quickly as possible. After thirty minutes, I had taken on so much spray that my camera cases were floating in the bottom of my boat. I was drenched and cold, but worst of all I couldn't see well enough to enjoy the scenery. After awhile the bay began to narrow, telling me the land cut was nearing. A few small islands began to break the incessant waves. Relief was in sight.

I leaped onto the dock at Guy Bailey's fishing camp, eager to feel something solid, then peeled my waterproof gear off. I couldn't find a single dry thread. Even my wallet was soaked, and the limp dollar bills inside looked like spoiled lettuce. Bailey, a big city dropout, rents a primitive bunkhouse and lighted fishing dock. His customers usually come in a float

Duck hunters slice through the silence of a sunrise over Garden Island Bay, Louisiana (overleaf).

Glasswort, a tiny succulent able to stand the supersaline condition at the edge of Laguna Madre

Blurred wings of black skimmers flitter across the setting sun at Timbalier Bay.

plane or a larger boat out to his isolated domain. Once a cook at the Houston Country Club, Bailey's special meals and excellent fishing draw celebrities and wealthy Texans to his humble docks.

After changing clothes, I searched the Padre Island dunes and sand flats for coyote tracks. I found some and, in spite of the wind, managed to assemble my blind. With a few rotten fish out as bait, I started playing the recorded call of a wounded jackrabbit, hoping a coyote would amble by. For two days I tried in three places, only to be outfoxed by the wily coyote. The gulls got the fish, a few jackrabbits hopped by, and a parade of clouds hinted that the weather didn't know what to do.

Surrounding my blind was an interesting plant, the glasswort, a salt-tolerant succulent able to survive the harsh bayside conditions. A ground-level macro view of these ten-inch plants looked like a giant juicy grove of trees with reddish trunks and lime green leaves.

The hypersaline condition of Laguna Madre is unique, though. Most Gulf Coast bays are more open and less saline like Apalachee Bay, Florida, which spreads before St. Marks National Wildlife Refuge.

From the St. Marks Lighthouse I watched a flapping, stretching congregation of birds on a nearby

Built in 1831, St. Marks Lighthouse overlooks Apalachee Bay.

A brown pelican sports his brilliant golden breeding feathers (right).

shell island exposed by low tide. More than a thousand cormorants mingled with a few gulls, terns, and pelicans. Red Giddens, the refuge biologist, and I walked out on the tidal flat where little spurts of water gave away the hiding place of buried mollusks.

Examining a piece of shoal grass, Red told me of a Corps of Engineers plan that would extend the intracoastal canal to within two miles of the refuge. Dredging and ship traffic would increase turbidity, threatening the sea grass community that feeds the world's second largest contingent of redhead ducks.

Behind us a sign in the middle of a pond reading ILLEGAL TO FEED THE ALLIGATORS piqued my curiosity. I asked Red why the 'gators were on a restricted diet.

"There's always people down here at the lighthouse and bayshore with a leftover chicken leg or a piece of bread," he said. "We were having a real problem last summer when a ten-foot 'gator started getting too friendly with the tourists. It got to the point where he lost his natural fear of humans and was aggressively coming for handouts. So we trapped him and carried him about three miles northeast of here to an area closed to the public. About two weeks later, I was down here and a little girl came up and told me a dead alligator was in the weeds. Sure enough, there was an

74

eight-foot 'gator with all four legs chewed off. Definitely done by another 'gator."

I asked Red if the one they had moved came back. "Yep," he said. "He came back, found that eight-footer in his territory getting all those handouts, and killed it. We trapped the big one again and carried him a long way off."

At St. Marks I also saw lots of deer and turkeys, a few bald eagles, and I saw a river otter crossing a small stream, but I never found the bobcat Red says he sees quite often.

Bays meant harbors to the New World explorers. The protection they offered from the rough waters of the open seas might be the reason a portion of Tampa Bay was named Safety Harbor. The bays that were safe harbors were found to be full of natural resources, and this led to the growth of big cities such as Corpus Christi, Houston, Mobile, Pensacola, and Tampa–St. Petersburg.

Flying over Tampa Bay early one morning, my first impression was that the Y-shaped bay had no room to breathe. Along the coast of St. Petersburg peninsula condominiums or subdivisions surrounded by seawalls are built right up to the beach. Most of the islands were linked to the mainland by causeways

A willet at sunset

Gulls in flight

Man's desire for beach-front recreation must be balanced with nature's need for wilderness coastline.

White pelicans lounge on a log in Mobile Bay.

Emptying into Choctawhatchee Bay, a creek forms a delta .

and dredged into two–car–one–boat homesites. Nevertheless, the two cities are nice: a harbor full of multicolored sailboats, the municipal pier and its free-loading pelicans, universities, cultural and sporting events, tourist attractions, and luckily, numbers of parks and wildlife refuges that make evident some semblance of the natural ecosystem. A bay must interact with some sand and vegetation.

Mobile Bay was discovered in 1519 by the Spanish explorer Alonso Alvarez de Pineda. When I reached it 474 years later I found winter trying to set in. Howling north winds were bringing frosty air that defied my long underwear and down jacket. My canoe suffered, too. I had placed sixty pounds of rocks in the front seat to keep the bow down and to help me navigate in gusty breezes as I paddled along the rim of the bay. I was trying to close in on some white pelicans that were resting on a tidal flat. Taking the long route and using tufts of wiregrass as wind buffers, I got close enough.

Once situated, I sank my hip boots and tripod into a couple of feet of mud and spent the rest of the day hiding behind my canoe as I photographed the pelicans.

As one of North America's largest birds, its wingspan can reach nine feet, or twenty inches more than

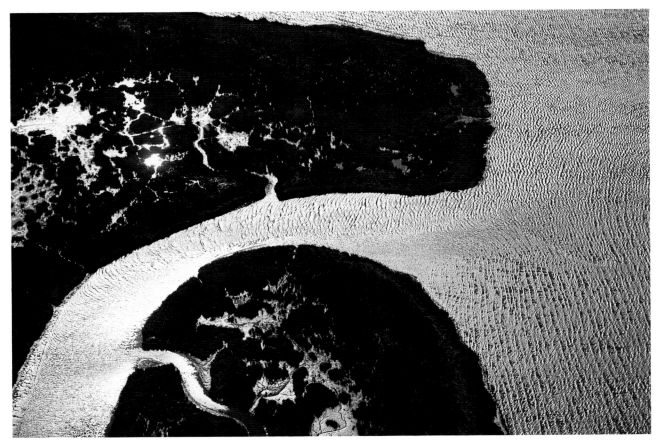

Proper salinity makes bays ideal oyster habitats.

that of its cousin the brown pelican. Whites winter in the fish-filled Gulf Coast bays then nest on desolate lake islands in the northern U.S. and Canada except for one small colony near Corpus Christi, Texas. During migration, the flocks are a spectacular sight as they flap and glide in a circle, riding the air currents. First they appear only white, then only black as they tilt, showing their wing tips, creating the same illusion as an optical puzzle.

From my cold, muddy spot, I watched a raccoon grab an oyster from a reef and slip into the marsh. Above, a potpourri of migrating birds was obviously being pushed south by the front. Flocks of gadwalls and widgeons winged overhead as small tight groups of teal zoomed low. Flights of dunlins, willets, and various sandpipers flushed and landed on the nearby mudbars, never bothering the rafts of coots that were pushing their bills through the inch-deep watery muck like miniature bulldozers.

Until the sun set behind the city of Mobile I stayed and watched the glow linger as it always does in new, clear cold air. Paddling out, the eerie call of the nutria, so humanlike, reminded me of a child crying.

Mobile Bay comprises about a third of Alabama's coast. It is bordered on the north by the productive

Oyster tongers work Apalachicola Bay.

Big Delta Swamp, whose Mobile and Tensaw rivers feed the bay with fresh water. The three-hundred-square-mile bay is nearly landlocked by the barrier beaches of Mobile Point and Dauphin Island where Fort Morgan and Fort Gaines protected the bay against Union ships during the Civil War.

On the western edge of the bay, boats hover over the oyster grounds. Unlike Louisiana fishermen, who use winch-operated oyster dredges, Alabama and Florida oystermen do it the hard way. Mechanical dredges are against the law in both states, so they must use oyster tongs, a scissorlike apparatus with a garden rake basket on the end. Strong-shouldered men stand on the decks of their small boats, pinching the tongs to dislodge and scoop up about a dozen oysters. They continue until enough sacks are filled to make the trip worthwhile, and the long days build massive shoulders on this vanishing breed of fisherman. I was glad to be lifting only a five-pound lens with the help of a tripod as I photographed these fellows in the glistening morning light.

Nearby Bayou La Batre, Alabama, is a seafood port that in 1981 brought in a catch worth $31,400,000, the tenth highest in the United States. With a relatively short coastline, Alabama offers many resources.

Louisiana ranks number one, having 3.3 million acres of bays in the coastal zone. Barataria is one of the most productive. It lies just west of the Mississippi and was historically nurtured by the river until the Corps of Engineers built the levees. It is still valuable, although it is losing ground due to the increasing saltwater intrusion caused by the Barataria waterway and other canals.

In late winter I visited Barataria Bay with John Day, coastal expert with the Louisiana State University Wetlands Resource Center. John showed me signs of the saltwater intrusion—dying trees and patches of wiregrass and oystergrass where cattails and bulltongue once grew. The salinity of this bay is very important to many marine organisms, particularly the oyster. Louisiana's 117,000 acres of oyster reefs depend on a delicate balance of salinity. With too much salt come predators like the drum fish. Another threat is the oyster drill, a predatory snail that attaches to the oyster, drills through its shell and eats the oyster. If the water is too fresh, the oyster will not survive.

I had heard the same thing from a Yugoslav oysterman, Dave Cvitanovich. Fishermen are now studying basic marine biology for an understanding of what

Bays provide a bounty of fish for recreation and survival.

Oystermen brave an Alabama downpour.

Great blue heron, Mississippi Sound (below)

East Bay, Louisiana, at sunset

keeps their catches in good health. Most of the large contingent of Croatian oystermen agree with John Day that Barataria Bay needs a freshwater transfusion from the Mississippi in order to remain productive.

Historically, the bay's rich bounty has attracted fishermen from around the world. That ethnic mix includes Chinese and Filipino emigrants who established enough stilt towns during the nineteenth century to win the name "Barataria's Asian Coast" for the area. We visited one stilt community, Manila Village, fifty years after it was abandoned because of storms and the advent of the motorboat. John pointed out that these fishermen settled as close as possible to their shrimping grounds, which explains why their homes hover above the marsh grass. Nearby was the shell mound of the bay's first inhabitants, the Houma Indians. In this kitchen midden of clam and oyster shells, I found some pottery shards. Most of these were indistinguishable from smooth stones, but I found a few with crude designs.

In lower Barataria Bay is Queen Bess Island where the Louisiana Department of Wildlife and Fisheries operates the successful brown pelican restocking program. The brown pelican, Louisiana's state bird, was extirpated from the state in the early 1960s when DDT and similar pesticides built up in the fat tissue of

85

Few fish escape the serrated bill of the red-breasted merganser.

A sandpiper casts a nearly perfect reflection while feeding.

the pelicans, resulting in death for many birds. Others laid eggs with shells so thin they never survived long enough to hatch. Restocking was begun in 1968 by the Department of Wildlife and Fisheries, and today over a thousand birds are nesting again.

A low-key Mount St. Helens: that's what I call Atchafalaya Bay. A geologic feat in the making. Geology is defined by time. It takes millions of years for some formations to mature, but at the bottom of the Atchafalaya Basin we are seeing a delta form in our lifetime. The Mississippi is locked in its channel, forming no new delta, and nowhere else in North America is one forming at the rate of the Atchafalaya Bay Delta.

In the 1950s, the bay was uniformly six feet deep. Big lakes in the upper Atchafalaya Basin were being filled by the 219,000 metric tons of sediment per day carried by the river. Once the lakes were full, the main sediment load rolled on past Morgan City, Louisiana, and out into the bay. Satellite photography discovered the first land in September, 1973, and by April, 1976, the bay had developed a substantial patch of emergent land. By 1979 the patch had grown to eleven square miles, and scientists at the Coastal Studies Institute of LSU predict eighty square miles of

Blue-wing teal erupt from a marsh pond in the Mississippi Delta.

land by the year 2030, which will extend the delta to the shell reefs at Point au Fer.

While the rest of the coast is losing land, Atchafalaya Bay is the bright spot in Louisiana coastal real estate. Even the ducks like it. The Louisiana Department of Wildlife and Fisheries aerial survey showed no noticeable use of the bay by puddle ducks in 1974. After the land appeared, the 1976 survey showed 100,000 puddle ducks wintering in the bay.

The new land will carve itself into smaller bays with islands and marsh, providing a diverse, more productive habitat for both man and wildlife.

4 The Islands

I wonder how long it will be before nature and man will accept each other again.

WALTER INGLIS ANDERSON

Walter Anderson, primitive artist, prolific journal keeper, explorer, potter, and eccentric, knew Horn Island, Mississippi, as few ever will. More than a hundred times he disappeared from the mainland in a rowboat or sailing skiff on three-week expeditions to paint the sun, sand, shells, pines, and pelicans. He traveled light, carrying one garbage can loaded with watercolors and paper, another full of food.

His food was only canned goods, rice, and the few fish he caught. His shelter was the skiff turned over on the beach. He filled his days wandering the beaches, sometimes naked, in search of subjects. Enduring the bites of insects, Anderson would crouch for hours to paint and observe a pelican nest, an anthill, or a wounded grebe.

The island was his passion. He wanted to be, and was, one with nature. To participate totally with the elements was his goal on the island, even to the extent of riding out Hurricane Betsy. Avoiding a Coast Guard team sent by his wife, he tied himself to a pine tree, then moved to a tall dune to outlast Betsy, which killed seventy-five people from Florida to Louisiana.

His peculiar habits branded him as a madman, and he was institutionalized several times of his own accord. After his death in 1965, five thousand neglected sketches and watercolors found under his bed won praise in the art world. These primitive renderings along with his journals were simple but significant. He wrote of halcyon days and moonlit nights. I saw them one November.

It was time for the hunter's moon and I waited for it in the cool air atop a tall dune. Dunes are the unstable stabilizing element in barrier islands—moving hills of sand. They shift with the wind and waves, holding an island intact so it can stand against raging storms, protecting the bays, marshes, and the man-made developments on the shore.

On Horn Island I moved carefully to avoid damaging dune vegetation, for even as the island depends on

Dune vegetation is the thread that holds the Gulf islands together.

the dune to maintain a reservoir of sand, the dune's existence depends on the success of plant life. Dunes are formed by blowing sand. Snaring airborne sand particles, a network of plants keeps the dune from blowing away. But only a few hardy plants can survive the sand, wind, and salt spray.

Surrounded by beach morning glory, sea oat, and scrub live oak, I watched the full moon stretch over the eastern end of Horn Island. When the moon got an angle on the island it was like a museum-quality duotone print, or more like a duotone movie. The white moon eased across the black sky spilling light on the waves as they licked the beach like silver tongues.

From my sandy perch, I watched cottontail rabbits zip from goldenrod patch to rosemary bush searching for tender vegetation, all the while avoiding the eyes and ears of a hungry owl.

That night at my campfire I was enjoying a muffin with honey when I noticed my backpack slowly disappearing into the thicket. My back and legs were sore from carrying the sixty-seven pounds of cameras, food, and gear in the soft sand for three days, but I wasn't about to let the trees swallow it all. I grabbed my end and pulled it out of the bushes with a young raccoon attached. He scurried away only to

Horn Island moonrise (right)

Red knots rest and preen on a Horn Island mud flat.

venture out fifteen minutes later with his brother and sister. Soon the three coons were eating the crumbs I had dropped. I squirted some honey in the sand and they gobbled it up, sand and all, until a growl from their mother called them back to the bushes. The next morning I found thousands of dainty footprints they had left while searching my campsite for more honey.

Three days earlier, when ranger Mark Holloman had dropped me off for my fourteen-mile hike along Horn Island, I learned that the island is creeping westward. During the past century littoral currents have moved the island three miles by sweeping sand off the east end and depositing it on the western tip. Neighboring Petit Bois Island (meaning small woods) lay partially in Alabama in the 1700s but now belongs exclusively to Mississippi.

Most of the sand in the Alabama and Mississippi barrier islands was carried by rivers from the southern Appalachian Mountains and emptied into the Gulf of Mexico. There are many theories about the formation of these islands, but it's generally agreed that storms, wind, currents, and the changing sea level of the last ice age are responsible for their beginning. Geologists call it longshore spit migration.

The older parts of the islands have dense vegetation where mosquitoes wait with hungry syringes. Not

As a wave approaches, a ghost crab anchors himself by his hole.

For the anatomy of an island compare this to the drawing on pages 4 and 5.

93

94   *Horn Island*

Yaupon adds autumn color.

wishing to sacrifice my blood that afternoon, I crossed to the open gulfside of the island where a black racer and a cottonmouth slid across my path.

Walking was easier on the hard beach sand, and I stopped occasionally to photograph a ghost crab (racing crab)—the crustacean escape artist. He blends so well with the sand that sometimes his lightning-fast shadow is the only thing that gives him away.

Using my tent as a blind, I watched one scurry from his hole above the high-tide line. Darting bravely toward the sea, he turned his side to an oncoming wave, anchored eight legs into the sand, and disappeared as the surf crashed over him. Emerging like Houdini, he grabbed a floating snack as the water was sucked back out to sea.

Birds can catch a young or sick crab occasionally, but the racing crab's nemesis is the feral hog. Working like a backhoe with cloven hoofs, the hog digs hard and deep for the pinching tidbit. All along the beach I found two-foot-deep holes revealing the nocturnal activities of these once domestic pigs.

Early settlers brought the hogs to many Gulf Coast islands where they escaped or were released to become wild. They have adapted supremely, competing with resident wildlife for the limited food supplies and endangering plant life by eating roots. Man's at-

95

Like silvery tongues, waves lick the Horn Island beach.

A black-bellied plover tugs at a stubborn worm.

tempts to hunt the hogs off the islands have failed.

As the sun slumped in the sky, I saw a large pleasure craft drop anchor on the island's landward side, and the next morning five people hiked across the island to play in the surf about a mile from my campsite. Eventually, a boy noticed my tent nestled in the dunes and jogged down the beach toward me. Out of breath he said, "Golly, isn't it great to be on an uninhabited island? How'd you get here!"

When I told him the ranger dropped me off for a four-day hike, his face lit up and he asked, "Man, you're out here just surviving?!"

I pointed to my pack. "I'm not exactly 'surviving'—there's food in there."

When I told him I had seen a school of two dozen porpoises, he jumped up and down with excitement.

"That's the only reason I came, to see porpoises. How far is it?" he yelled back as he flew down the beach with dreams of porpoises and castaways at his heels.

That afternoon I packed my gear and my contented soul into the boat of Dr. William Walker, a fisheries biologist at the Gulf Coast Research Laboratories. I took with me memories of shimmering moonlit beaches and sandpiper tracks melting under gentle waves. The enchanting blend of wind-bent oaks and

Raccoon tracks near the author's campsite, Horn Island

Dauphin Island camps have been rebuilt since Hurricane Frederic ravaged the island in 1979.

mounds of sculptured sand faded as I left the crown jewel of Mississippi's gold coast. And I understood Walter Anderson's island romance.

On the solid but swaying pilings of Hunter Horgan's Dauphin Island, Alabama, camp I sat out the first norther of the winter. The forty-mph winds rattled the shutters as the temperature dropped into the thirties.

Grateful that I wasn't camping in my leaky tent, I dared to remember a night in 1972 when the accommodations weren't so cozy. While filming wildlife off the Texas coast, Marty Stouffer, the wildlife filmmaker, his assistant, David Huie, and I had set up camp on a clump of shells and sand no bigger than an acre. With our camera gear and food secured in the supply tent, we innocently settled into our down sleeping bags that chilly spring evening for what would be the wildest night of our lives. The winds mounted, and water sloshed as waves broke over the island. Then the winds began to rage. We shivered in our submerged sleeping bags (the feathers now like yesterday's oatmeal) as camera cases floated about in the supply tent. We waited out the long night, praying for daylight and, most of all, for life. When we learned later that winds had reached seventy mph we knew our prayers had been heard.

Constant sea breezes bend Horn Island oaks (preceding page).

A royal tern guards her nest at a Timbalier Island rookery.

Actually, I was foolish to count on being cozy, for Dauphin Island is no stranger to storms. On September 12, 1979, Hurricane Frederic boiled over the island with winds of 130 mph, crumbling $22 million worth of homes, camps, motels, curio shops, and bridges. These man-made structures suffered, but the island, that unstable mass of sand, bent with the storm and survived.

Just three years later, lumber trucks were now rolling over the $34 million causeway with supplies for reconstruction. Every year this part of the coast faces a 13 percent chance of being hit hard by a hurricane, and it is amazing how quickly owners are willing to rebuild.

Ironically, the federal government encourages rebuilding by maintaining conflicting policies. Barrier islands are protected through the National Seashore and National Wildlife Refuge systems. Both state and federal governments have dune-rebuilding and island-erosion programs. Yet the federal government heavily subsidizes development of barrier islands by financing highways and bridges—cement links to the mainland. Uncle Sam doles out millions for sewer and water lines that traverse the bridges along with scores of tourists and settlers. As if land access weren't enough,

102   *A willet walks at sunset on a St. Petersburg beach.*

When all of an island's dunes are developed, its natural resilience

Coastal zone management teams hope to control man's impact on the fragile Gulf Coast ecosystem.

after storms is lost.

the Corps of Engineers carves out harbors and dredges channels to provide a liquid avenue for Chris Crafts, crew boats, and trawlers.

When a hurricane finally obliterates the structures, the government assuages landowners' griefs with federal insurance monies so they can rebuild before the next storm. Perhaps pending legislation will put an end to these senseless outlays. But some islands are now irretrievably buried beneath concrete and condos; for example, Destin Beach, Florida. From my childhood trips to the sleepy fishing village of Destin, I recall only a few motels, none of them on the barrier beach. Today multistory condo complexes stretch toward the sun that millions flock to worship, beginning at Easter each year. In those earlier days swimming, fishing, or beachcombing entertained us. Now vacationers expect discos, parasailing, and a tangle of concrete dragons disguising a putt-putt golf course for amusement.

It is not easy for a naturalist to understand the dichotomy that exists in Florida's land use. Beaches are heavily developed for commercial purposes; at the same time the state boasts more protected park and refuge land than any other Gulf Coast state. Florida has the nation's largest fleet of barrier islands, guard-

Abandoned pier, South Pass, Mississippi River

Chandeleur Lighthouse is the only development on the forty-mile chain of islands.

ing the mainland like lazy soldiers strung along the mouths of rivers where constant regurgitation of sediment provides the nourishment for survival.

Island-hopping Florida's coast reveals variety and contrast that belie the stereotype of sand, palms, and octogenarians.

Not far from Apalachicola where the panhandle heads southward, a wedge of land was acquired by the Florida Fish and Wildlife Service in 1968. St. Vincent Island was once the hunting preserve of Dr. R. V. Pierce, a patent medicine king of the early twentieth century. In those days Dr. Pierce imported zebra, eland, black buck, and sambur deer, which strolled beneath the stately live oaks and nibbled tender new shoots in the jungle of understory. Now all but the sambur deer have been relocated in zoos.

I toured St. Vincent with a French television documentary crew and Robert Gray, a refuge employee. The multitude of flora on the slice of sand was incredible. From the Gulf beach, salty rivulets snaked their way toward the interior where mature moss-draped oaks anchored ancient dunes.

I shinnied my way up the trunk of an oak past pink lichens and miniature ferns that sprouted from the bark. Looking north, I saw brown stems of cattails bent over in a violet-blue lake rimmed with cabbage

Typical island ridges are covered with lichen-dressed oaks.

Among the varied habitat of St. Vincent Island is palmetto and slash-pine forest (right).

palm. In a nearby dead palm three large holes had been knocked out by nesting woodpeckers. Behind me the view was a jagged crop of vibrant green palmetto fronds backlit by the afternoon sun.

We saw various ducks, a black racer, a Gulf Coast box turtle, and the fleeting shape of a sambur deer as our jeep rumbled along the earthen trail toward the beach. As I lay on the warm sand, I watched hundreds of small coon oysters exposed by low tide. Robert casually pried one open with his old notched penknife and pretty soon the nine of us were eating them faster than he could shuck.

Around the bend and just south of the Suwannee River is Seahorse Key, a lump of a thing that rises to fifty-four feet in a breadth of only three hundred yards. I call a hill *steep* if walking down is as hard as walking up, and I had many occasions to travel that hill during my rainy three days on the island.

At the apex of Seahorse is an old Coast Guard lighthouse where I sat in the octagonal tower watching ospreys through watery windowpanes. Seven pairs were gathering sticks to build their loosely stacked nests, one in a man-made box, the rest in live oaks and palms. A group of brown pelicans also nests there, but only a handful compared to the colony

Cabbage palms line a freshwater lake on St. Vincent Island.

monitored by refuge manager Bob Ziobro in Tampa Bay.

Bob took me out to Tarpon Key, a mangrove atoll that supports the country's largest or second-largest pelican rookery, varying from year to year. It was only mid-February, but already a thousand birds were carrying sticks and grass for nest-building. Ziobro's territory includes nine islands in Tampa Bay that provide nesting grounds for tens of thousands of birds including the black oyster-catcher.

Egmont Key has no major rookery but is critical habitat for the Florida gopher tortoise. Dodging tortoise dens and potholes in a brick road through the World War II army base, Bob showed me a century plant. After growing dagger-tipped leaves for many years (never a full century), it sends a single stalk toward the sky, sometimes thirty-five feet tall. In a final burst of energy, a magnificent creamy flower appears, containing seeds. Then the plant dies.

On the Gulf beach of Egmont we found a smorgasbord of shells, many in perfect condition. As far up as the high-tide line were millions of shells washed ashore in a recent storm.

Beaches from Tampa Bay to Marco Island are considered prime hunting grounds for shell collectors. Across a three-dollar toll bridge near Fort Myers is

Florida's west coast supports a healthy population of osprey.

Sanibel Island, the shell capital of America; it ranks fifth in the world.

Fresh water from the Caloosahatchee River bathes the island, attracting fresh, brackish, and saltwater shell species. The only east-west-oriented barrier island on Florida's west coast, it is surrounded by curling currents that deposit tons of shells. So good is the shelling that there are more shell hunters bent over like hairpins than sunbathers or swimmers.

Although Sanibel is rather highly developed, it was zoned to prohibit construction over two stories high, leaving the skyline unobstructed. A special feature of the island is the 4,833-acre J. N. "Ding" Darling National Wildlife Refuge, which draws more visitors than any other Gulf Coast refuge and offers winter residence to a broad assortment of migratory birds (see Appendix C). Among the forty-seven species I saw in one afternoon was a laughing gull perched unsteadily on the head of a swimming brown pelican. As the pelican ducked under and emerged with a fish, the gull bent and bobbed to steal the meal.

Unlike Sanibel, little planning went into Marco Island, and as a consequence its row of fourteen high-rise condos looks more like New York City than a tropical island.

The fifty-mile stretch of coastline below Marco Is-

Shells from along the coast

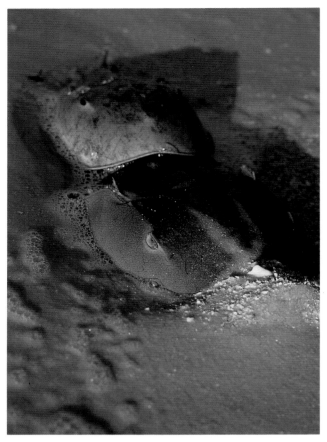

Horseshoe crabs mate on Rabbit Key.

land is dotted with a myriad of mangrove clumps known as Ten Thousand Islands. It is the western boundary of the Everglades, with names like Faka-hatchee River, Chokoloskee Bay, Sandfly Pass, and Mosquito Key.

There were no signs of rabbits on Rabbit Key where I camped, but at low tide a sandbar extending from the eastern end of the island did resemble rabbit ears.

I arrived on a rising tide and had to search for a place to pull ashore without crushing a group of breeding horseshoe crabs. Not a true crab, but an ar-thropod kin to the spider, the horseshoe has been around for 360 million years performing its spring-time ritual without fail. When a full or new moon brings the month's highest tide, the female crawls to the high-tide line dragging up to a dozen males. There she lays her eggs, which will incubate for two weeks and hatch in the warm sand before the tide climbs to this level again and gently washes the hatchlings out to sea.

The sun and moon millions of miles away control the tides, which affect the life cycles of many seashore plants and animals. For example the red mangrove produces cigar-shaped propagules that drop from its

At high tide submerged roots of the red mangrove offer refuge to small fish.

Receding tides expose the prop roots and surrounding mud flats, which lure feeding birds.

branches. At low tide a seedling may be able to stick right into the mud and begin root formation, however high tide can float it away, and eventually it may find another tidal flat and take root.

In this way shallow tidal flats become mangrove colonies where dozens of spindly legs called prop roots arch into water from each tree. Sand carried by the tides is trapped by the prop roots in a land-building process that eventually forms mangrove islands. These islands provide nurseries for various forms of aquatic life.

With mask, snorkle, and underwater camera, I photographed a true "fisheye" view of the prop root community. Darting in and out of the alga-covered roots, a school of a thousand minnows was being chased by a playful ten-inch barracuda. Grey snapper and other juvenile fish seek refuge here from larger fish of the reefs. Nestled in the surrounding turtle grass were translucent anemones, their purple-tipped arms waving slowly in the surge, and sea cucumbers like overgrown wrinkled slugs covered with brown felt.

Some land animals also rely on the ceaseless wash of the tides. Flocks of willets, sandpipers, dunlins, plovers, sanderlings, and gulls synchronize their appetites with the receding tides and probe the exposed

American oyster catcher

Biologist Jake Valentine counts tern nests.

flats for oysters, whelks, tiny black snails, and worms. Flushing in complex formations, the peeps, as small shorebirds are called, zoomed off to another tidal flat as we left for the Keys.

United States Highway 1 threads more than one hundred miles of the Florida Keys together, arching its asphalt ribbon over as much water as land. This mixture of limestone, mangroves, and sand is critical habitat for many endangered species. Small portions of the Everglades and the Keys are the only places to find the American crocodile. The hundreds of mangrove islets in Florida Bay are prime nesting habitats for the southern bald eagle. Other endangered species in the Keys include the great white heron, brown pelican, and the key deer. This minuscule relative of the white-tail deer has been befriended and fed by the residents of Big Pine Key, causing it to lose its fear of man and too often to become a traffic fatality. About forty key deer are smashed on the highway each year.

On Big Pine Key one small subdivision is known for its key deer parties held at sunset. The crepuscular deer come for handouts, and the people come to watch or to illegally feed North America's smallest ungulate. On the evening I went, seven carloads attended, most with handfuls of food. A white-haired lady in a pink dress told me, as she bent over to hand

A stately great egret on Sanibel Island

Snails feed at low tide on Rabbit Key.

a piece of white bread to a doe, that she also goes over to No Name Key to feed the raccoons. Behind her a sign read FEEDING KEY DEER ILLEGAL, VIOLATORS SUBJECT TO FINE. At sunrise I found a buck browsing in the pines and palmettos. It amazed me that his six-point antlers barely topped my belt.

Highway 1 ends at Key West, a colorful tourist town where drinking at Ernest Hemingway's favorite bar and applauding the sunset with local residents is a daily ritual. Most travelers have no idea that the waters between Key West and Dry Tortugas support an eighteen-million-pound-per-year pink shrimp industry, a fishery happened upon during a lucky breakdown.

In 1945 a lone fisherman set his nets out to stabilize his boat in the waves while he repaired his engine. On pulling the nets, he found to his surprise that they were laden with pink shrimp. Reportedly, he tried to keep the new fishing grounds a secret, but soon boats followed him and discovered his bonanza.

Few tourists ever get to see the Tortugas, which offer excellent reefs for the scuba diver. There is also Fort Jefferson for the history buff, and rare terns for the bird watcher.

The brown noddy and sooty tern both nest here in large colonies, but nothing like the thirty thousand

Key deer forage for mangrove seeds.

sandwich terns Jake Valentine counted at the Chandeleur Island nesting colony off Louisiana. Jake doesn't really count the flying birds, but uses a formula devised from over thirty years of counting for the Fish and Wildlife Service. His method involves multiplying the number of nests per square foot by the length and width of the colony.

For three days I scampered ahead, cameras clanking about my neck, to gaze patiently through a telephoto lens at Jake and his helpers as they counted almost connecting colonies of skimmers, gulls, pelicans, herons, egrets, ibises, and terns. It was in $\frac{1}{250}$ of a second that I finally framed Jake's wind-worn and sun-scorched face as the multitudes of sandwich terns flushed in front of him.

About 75,000 colonial birds nest on the Chandeleur Islands and another 847,000 along the entire coast of Louisiana. Most of these homemakers choose barren sand spits of deteriorating barrier islands to dig the shallow depressions they use for nests. The sparseness of vegetation makes it inhospitable for raccoons and other predators, including man. I knew this only too well from the previous summer when I watched another colony of terns on a similar mound of sand and shells in Timbalier Bay.

Blackbirds are excluded from the Florida law forbidding the picking of sea oats.

Royal terns circle their nesting colony (above and overleaf).

Once a week for the entire summer I set up my blind among the terns and periodically tried to observe them while I also swatted deer flies at my ankles and scratched sand-flea bites on my head. The thrill of watching the terns throughout their life cycle of courtship, nest building, egg laying, and hatching and feeding the young made the insects and the sauna-like heat of my movable brown double-knit blind almost bearable.

One other thing makes the birds choose these barrier islands for nesting sites: food. The precocious little terns need lots of fish. They require so much that a few adults guard a nursery pod of fifty to seventy-five chicks while the other adults repeatedly plunge into the Gulf for baby mullet and other silvery minnows. With its catch clasped firmly in its tiny beak the parent hovers over the pod somehow detecting the chirp of its own amongst the cacophony. With my ears ringing, I finished each day with the visual reward of flittering tern wings painting a tapestry of motion across the setting sun.

Not all Louisiana's barrier islands are as barren as the tern nesting sites; some are younger, with more vegetation. It's a matter of age. All of Louisiana's barrier islands were formed by the changing deltas of the Mississippi River. They start with an active delta and

As part of their nesting ritual, black skimmers court with a fish.

Vines of the beach morning glory help anchor the dunes.

Louisiana has had five such deltas in the last six thousand years. When the river moves, the previous delta begins to erode making a small bay behind the delta tip. Soon the bay grows landward and larger, forming an arc of barrier islands such as the Chandeleurs, finally sinking into the Gulf to form a shoal.

Now that the Corps of Engineers has put controls on the Mississippi River, there will be no new deltas and no new islands. There are predictions that Isle Derniere will last 35 to 50 years and the Chandeleurs will last 60 to 350 years.

In the normal scheme of things this would be all right; a shoal is valuable habitat too. But with no new islands being formed, the marshland is in jeopardy; there are no roving spits of sand to protect them.

Can we stop the subsidences of these barriers? Probably not, but we can slow it down. Just as a bankrupt company needs dollars, a sandrupt island needs sand. Too many times the planners, engineers, and politicians overlook this and go to more expensive, less aesthetic, and grossly ineffective methods of putting rocks or seawalls on the eroding beaches. Only to find out later that storms can move rocks just as easily as they move sand. Sand and the proper dune plants can hold these islands together a lot longer and

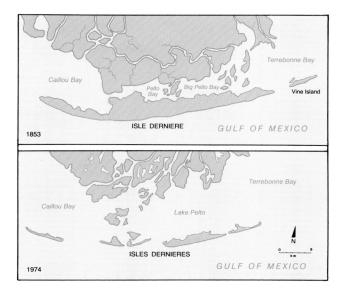

In only 121 years Isle Derniere eroded from a substantial 38-mile-long barrier island to a minor string of islets.

MAP 3   Isles Dernieres Barrier System, 1853 and 1974

Pelicans and egrets drift toward their rookery on Queen Bess Island.

A sunset for Walter Anderson

a lot cheaper than any other method tried to date.

To a boy an island is a dream, a place of adventure where treasure lies waiting beneath the sand, where bands of pirates made their last stand. To Walter Anderson it meant a romance with the wildlife. To the coast, an island is a critical piece of the puzzle that makes the deep blue waters of the Gulf work efficiently with the bays and marshes.

5 The Deep Blue

The clear blue water is frothing in a feeding frenzy as sharks, lings, bonita, and amberjacks tear into the trash dumped overboard from the trawler *Lucky Lady*. The trash is tons of unwanted fish, crabs, and other aquatic creatures that the shrimper drags up inadvertently in his nets.

Our boat pulls closer to watch the frantic sharks, so thick I imagine walking across the water on their backs. I climb aboard the trawler and see three men, with the typical tattoos and white rubber boots, trademarks of Louisiana fishermen. The men are bent over grabbing and beheading jumbo brown shrimp, with speed and ease only years of experience can bring. Seafood is heaped about four feet deep and covers the entire stern deck of the ninety-five-foot shrimp boat.

As I stand knee-deep in the wiggling mass of fish flesh I muse: A drop of rain rolls off the bank of the meandering Mississippi River in northern Minnesota. Picking up a piece of sediment, it makes the long journey downriver, through swamp, across marsh and bay to help build up one of the world's most prolific fisheries systems in the Gulf of Mexico.

Shrimp is the most valuable seafood commodity in the American harvest and 75 percent, or $401,400,000 worth, are caught in the Gulf of Mexico. The Gulf also leads in quantity of fish. In 1982 about 58 percent of the 2,105,409,000 pounds of menhaden were caught in Gulf waters, mainly off Louisiana and Mississippi. Waters nurtured by 17,141 miles of shoreline, numerous bays, and endless marshes make an ideal ecosystem for all sorts of marine animals.

The *Lucky Lady* is drawing a crowd, now. Seven fishing boats are drifting about trying to entice one of the lings with lures and baits. Back in our boat we head for a petroleum platform to get a firsthand view of what the deep blue looks like from underneath.

There are no waves today. In fact the water is so slick and calm that through the hot, hazy July air I can't tell where the sky begins. In my wet suit, I heat up quickly, so I pour a bucket of cool Gulf water into my suit before putting on my tank. Then, tank secure, air on, gauges OK, camera in hand, I waddle penguin style to the bow of the boat and jump

A lone shrimp boat trawls the Gulf waters.

scissor-legged into three hundred feet of ink blue water.

Sinking slowly along one of the massive steel legs of Shell Oil's platform 152 West Delta, I gaze down through one hundred feet of liquid space. Surf fishermen in the muddy green water off Grand Isle never believe how clear it can get out here.

The usually guarded barracuda swims by to check me out, and I notice six more patrolling their territory in a corner of the rig. I swim toward the center, and the 'cudas get out of my way as the massive platform above shades out the sun.

Sinking, sinking. At twenty feet, five hundred pancake-flat fish swim toward me. A few feet away the plate-sized fish turn to show me their silver sides; my strobe light bounces off them like tin foil. They're called lookdowns—an appropriate name, for their eyes seem to be forever fixed on the ocean floor far below.

Deeper I drift. I am at amberjack level where thirty of the fleshy, powerful swimmers circle me like I'm a wagon train. The biggest one looks like a fifty-pounder. The jack cravelle mingle with schools of snapper at one hundred feet. Looking up I have an eerie feeling, like being in a giant cathedral with arching roof-top and stained-glass windows. Shafts of sun-

Depending on the winds and currents, waters off the coast of Louisiana range from eerie green (above) to crystal-clear blue (below).

light penetrate the edges as all of those fish swim above like angels in the sky.

In front of me the vertical drill pipes are so well covered with a soft coral, *Telesto* sp., that the six-foot space between them is nearly breached by the tentacle-tipped arms of the coral.

Up ahead I see the whiplike movements of spiny lobster antennae. The lobster senses my presence and crawls partially out of the coral to feel my vibrations. I check my strobe and frame the shot as five species of fish swim out from behind the coral. The queen angelfish, spotfin butterfly fish, creole fish, brown chromis, and squirrelfish along with the coral and lobster make me forget I am under an oil rig. This looks like a Caribbean reef.

Floating back toward the surface with my tropical photographs, my eyes are still wide with awe. After hundreds of dives I still see new things, an Atlantic thorny oyster, for instance, its shell, studded with beautiful orange and ivory spines, opening to release cloud after cloud of sperm. Or a tiny freckled blenny darting in and out of its dead barnacle home. On many dives I have watched these colorful fish for hours; their comical faces take on a look of panic until they get used to my hulking presence. Then they're

Gray snapper rely on the small coral heads for protection in the

A telesto, a gorgonian with tiny arms extended, snags a plankton as it drifts by in the currents.

126

Florida Keys.

back to normal, rocketing out of their barnacle to grab a passing piece of food, diving headfirst back into their home, and turning around instantly to guard the entrance.

In contrast to the tiny blenny are the jewfishes, or big groupers, as the larger ones are affectionately called. What a thrill it was to peer around a piling at fifty feet and see three of these monsters. They reminded me of Volkswagens. A couple of two-hundred-pounders were next to a big grouper longer than I am and weighing at least six hundred pounds. It could have swallowed me, but I took my chances and swam up to pet him. (All big jewfishes and groupers are males; the females turn into males at a certain size.) This one didn't like my company and turned to dive. The propwash from his tail pushed me back four feet and knocked my mask up on my forehead. He had power and bulk that would make a shark take notice.

I have endless tales of sharks, sea turtles, manta rays, tarpons, and other spectacular sea creatures that travel the Gulf waters. Many of them visit the oil rigs where little creepy crawlers stick close to the artificial reef habitat. And there are a lot of rigs; so many in fact, that one evening at the Mississippi's South Pass

An inch-long blenny makes its home in a dead barnacle.

127

Schools of silver-sided, pancake-thin lookdowns sometimes number in the thousands.

129

Deep beneath an oil rig, tropical fish swim between the gorgonian-covered stanchions.

On the surface at night a flying fish rests with fins outstretched.

when I took the *National Geographic* writer Doug Lee atop my houseboat, he asked if the hundreds of oil rigs in East Bay were the lights of some city.

In the northern Gulf of Mexico, 3,342 petroleum structures form 3,750 acres of artificial reef habitat. Fishermen, divers, and reef-dwelling creatures benefit. But what about the environment as a whole? From my observations most of the rigs do little damage to the deep blue. Aside from a few slipshod drilling operators who let exorbitant amounts of drilling mud, chemicals, oil, gas, paint, detergent, sewage, and garbage fall into the Gulf, most rigs are run conscientiously.

It's the industry that services offshore rigs that creates a problem. Along coastal Louisiana, shrimp and oyster villages of fifty years ago have become oil boomtowns. Four-engine crew boats roar down manmade canals through the once quiet marsh. Bays and bayous are dredged and lined with pilings, pipelines, and storage tanks. It's too bad the marsh is neglected, because the Gulf's 615,384 square miles of water surface, larger than the state of Alaska, cannot soak up pollution forever.

The greatest threat is another supertanker oil spill as formidable as Ixtoc in Mexico. Here the Gulf's shoreline would be in immediate jeopardy as tides, wind,

The tricolor anemone protects the flat-clawed hermit crab while scraps from the crab's food provide meals for the anemone.

Coco damselfish

and currents pushed oil onto the beaches and through the marshes, endangering aquatic nursery grounds. Breeding fishes in the estuaries would fail to produce offspring to replenish the deep blue.

The depth of the Gulf averages about 5,000 feet, but at its deepest point (12,598 feet) it would take ten Empire State buildings with a California redwood on top to break the surface of its rolling waves. This multibillion-gallon waterhole receives life-giving input from two sources. Tropical Caribbean waters enter the Gulf through the 100-mile wide Yucatan Channel, circulate through the Gulf, and exit between Cuba and Florida. A more important water source is the freshwater runoff from two-thirds of the United States and one-half of Mexico. The effects of these waters divide the Gulf into a terrigenous, or muddy, zone in the west and a carbonate, or dead, reef zone in the east.

The terrigenous zone lies mainly off the shores of Texas and Louisiana and is divided into three habitats, of which two are estuarine dependent. The white shrimp grounds include the shoreline out to a depth of 66 feet, and the brown shrimp grounds go from 66 to 330 feet. The third habitat is the outer shelf area, which is tropical since it gets a lot of Caribbean water from the Yucatan Channel. Being farther south and deeper, the temperature stays warmer year-around allowing for tropical species.

Out there is where the big fish play. Ten-ton whale sharks, sailfish, and the highly prized blue marlin, synonym for power.

To get a feel for this deep blue habitat, some friends and I arranged another diving expedition, this time with our shark cage. We stacked our 6-by-7-by-7-foot cage on Rusty Wharton's 33-foot outboard boat. We had six enthusiastic men, fifty-five scuba tanks, lots of cameras, and buckets of blood from the local slaughterhouse with which to entice the sharks.

Ready for three days of shark photography, we left Grand Isle for a 70-mile journey in search of a riptide. A rip or grass line is one of the most interesting habitats in the deeper waters. Differing currents, water densities, and temperatures cause two adjacent bodies of water to form a line of sargassum weed and various forms of flotsam. This junction can be a line 4 to 50 feet wide and sometimes 50 miles long.

Within the sticky yellow sargassum weed, its bb-like air bladders keeping it afloat, is a miniature ecosystem. Here strange creatures like the sargassum fish blend in perfect camouflage with their drifting home. Others that also blend are species of shrimp, nudi-

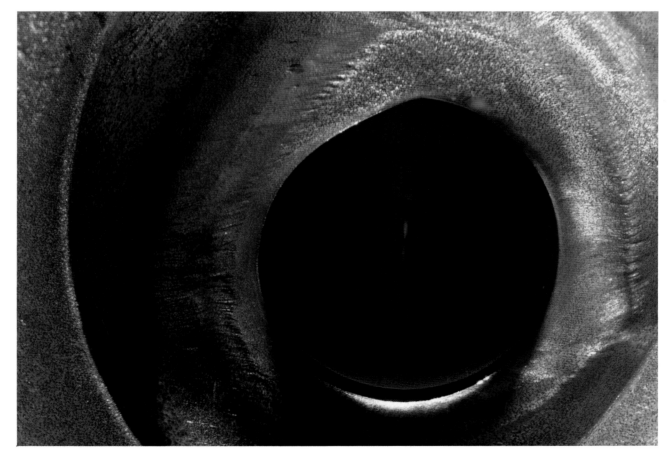

The eye of a red snapper

Star coral offshore near Cocodrie, Louisiana

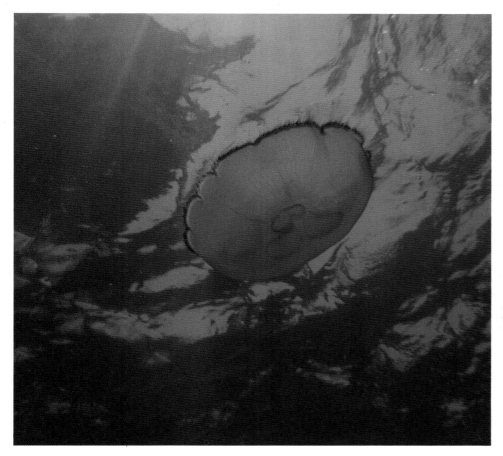

This jellyfish, like the immobile coral, is a colony of minute single-celled animals.

The white-tailed tropic bird is an infrequent visitor to the Florida Keys.

branch, and filefish. Below the grass line are larger fish such as young amberjack and school dolphin which swim below and wait for one of the camouflage fish to make a mistake. The grass is also used by these fish for shade and for protection from sharks and marlin.

After three hours of the cage banging on the bowrail we found a rip with blue water on both sides. According to our charts, it was 2,000 feet to the bottom where the big sharks live. And we wanted big sharks—because the little ones, up to 6 feet long, could swim right through the bars of our homemade cage. Once while out with a marlin fisherman, I had seen 12-to-14-foot hammerhead sharks cruising the rip. That's what we wanted.

It took all six of us to slide the cage into the Gulf. Soon we had our chum line working and our underwater speaker sending out sharklike signals—sounds we made in a radio studio with a "white noise generator," rapid and irregular pules that sharks are supposed to like. Then the cage was ready to submerge. Everything looked perfect, another flat calm day that Gulf fishermen dream about.

We were drifting on the bluer side of the rip. Warm gin-clear blue water rubbing against colder blue-green water on the north side of the grass line. Leaping into

The abandoned Little Pass Lighthouse lies off East Timbalier Island (right).

One of the small blacktip sharks the author encountered from his shark cage

The arrowhead crab gets its name from its pointed head.

the water I looked down, but there was no reference point just blue, bluer, bluest water going down, down, down toward a muddy bottom I could never see. I swam toward the cage and saw a beautiful sleek dolphin swimming in the pea-soup-colored water under the sargassum grass. Where the two waters met it formed a yucky color; I could see heat waves in it like a desert mirage.

Before I could get to the cage, a four-foot blacktip shark cruised by and nipped at my flipper. I ducked into the cage and the shark swam right through. Blood from the chum line turned blue as it hit the salt water and drifted by the cage. Soon Wayne Bettoney, Phil Cohagen, and I were swimming outside of the cage while three young blacktip sharks swam through the cage.

For three days we drifted in the riptide, never getting more than four sharks in sight at one time and never getting one bigger than five feet long. Still we all enjoyed getting to know the deep-water community a little better.

Texas boasts the northernmost coral reefs in the Gulf of Mexico. Jutting up like mother ocean's breasts are two salt domes 110 miles southeast of Galveston. Millions of years ago when these domes flowed upward, they carried up enough rock to form the hard

Colonies of anemones attach themselves to coral reefs and oil-rig stanchions (left).

137

Night falls on a set of oil platforms forty miles off the Louisiana coast.

substrate that phytontic coral offspring needed to start a colony. Now, after years of building, these two pinnacles reach within 60 feet of the surface, displaying colorful corals, sponges, tube worms, and tropical fish in an array deserving of their name—the Flower Gardens Reef.

Reefs this beautiful and bountiful are usually found in Florida waters, the carbonate zone of the Gulf. Caribbean waters combined with very little freshwater runoff to make this bottom of sand, limestone, and ancient coral reef.

Waters off the west coast of Florida deepen very gradually; in fact the rule is about one foot per mile offshore. Sixty miles off Grand Isle, Louisiana, the depth is two thousand feet, but you'll find only sixty feet of water at the same distance off Cedar Key, Florida.

Cracks and sinkholes in this hard bottom create habitat for lobster and grouper, making Florida the leading Gulf state in providing lobster and finfish for human consumption.

In the Keys and Dry Tortugas where the water is even warmer, still more diversity exists in the coral communities. The coral also grows much bigger than the small patches on the oil rigs.

From the Tortugas to Brownsville, Texas, and

Waters from two-thirds of the United States pour out from the Mississippi at Southwest Pass.

Orange fireworm

from the headwaters of the Mississippi River to the bottom of the Gulf, every drop of water works to form one of the most interesting and productive habitats in the world.

Appendices

APPENDIX A
Gulf of Mexico Facts

WATER

Surface Area	615,384 square miles
Maximum Depth	12,598 feet

COASTAL MILEAGE

	Coastline[1]	Shoreline[2]
United States	12,383 miles	88,633
Gulf Coast	1,631 (13%)	17,141 (19%)
Texas	367	3,359
Louisiana	397	7,721
Mississippi	44	359
Alabama	53	607
Florida	770	5,095

[1] General length of the coast

[2] The length of the coast as well as that of islands, bays, rivers, and creeks up to the head of tidewater

BARRIER ISLANDS

	Area (acres)	Miles of undeveloped beach (not including refuges)
Texas	383,953,000	150
Louisiana	38,518,000	79
Mississippi	9,727,000	9
Alabama	28,213,000	14
Florida	518,933,000★	72

★ Includes Atlantic coast

MARSH

	Acres	
Texas	397,917	6%
Louisiana	2,625,363	41%
Mississippi	66,937	1%
Alabama	11,856	1%
Florida	921,804	14%
U.S. Gulf	4,023,877	63%
Remaining continental U.S. coast	2,403,557	37%

PROTECTED WATER AREA (bays, ponds, etc.)

	Acres
Texas	1,532,430
Louisiana	3,378,924
Mississippi	500,379
Alabama	397,353
Florida	2,081,525
TOTAL	7,890,611

OYSTER REEFS

	Acres
Texas	12,477
Louisiana	117,518
Mississippi	9,786
Alabama	5,038
Florida	13,844
TOTAL	158,663

MISSISSIPPI RIVER DELTAS

Delta	Years before present
Maringouin Complex	7200–6200
Teche	5800–3900
St. Bernard	4700–700
Lafourche	3500–75
Plaquemine	1000–present

Gulf Coast State Parks

LOUISIANA

Sam Houston Jones State Park
Route 4, Box 294
Lake Charles, La. 70601
(318) 855-2665
Features several lagoons; many nature trails in wooded area.

Longfellow-Evangeline State Commemorative Area
P.O: Box 497
St. Martinville, La. 70582
(318) 394-3754
Late-18th-century Acadian house; Acadian craft shop.

Cypremort Point State Park
Star Route B, Box 428AA
Franklin, La. 70538
(318) 867-4510
Access to Gulf; man-made beach in a natural marsh with fresh- and saltwater fishing.

Edward Douglass White State Commemorative Area
RFD 2, Box 234
Thibodaux, La. 70301
(504) 447-3473
130-year-old homestead of former statesman and Chief Justice of the U.S. Supreme Court E. D. White

Grand Isle State Park
P.O. Box 741
Grand Isle, La. 70358
(504) 787-2559
Access to Gulf, beach, and fishing jetties.

St. Bernard State Park
P.O. Box 534
Violet, La. 70092
(504) 682-2101
On Mississippi; man-made lagoons with canoeing and fishing; located near Chalmette National Historical Park and New Orleans.

Fort Pike State Commemorative Area
Route 6, Box 194
New Orleans, La. 70129
(504) 662-5703
Fort used in War of 1812; near Old Spanish Trail and 23 miles east of downtown New Orleans.

Fontainebleau State Park
P.O. Box 152
Mandeville, La. 70448
(504) 626-8052
On Lake Pontchartrain; nature trails; ruins of plantation brickyard and sugar mill.

MISSISSIPPI

Buccaneer State Park
P.O. Box 180
Waveland, Miss. 39576
(601) 467-3822
Located on Gulf; excellent campground; popular attraction: wavepool; nature trail with elevated observatory; fishing in Gulf; one of most popular parks in system.

Gulf Marine State Park
P.O. Box 433
Biloxi, Miss. 39533
(601) 435-4355
Open for fishing, crabbing, shrimping from piers on 24-hour basis; a park interpretative center featuring marine science displays; picnicking and sunning on piers and decks.

Shepard State Park
1100 Graveline Rd.
Gautier, Miss. 39553
(601) 435-4355
Still in development stage: a 400-acre park on former pine-tree farm; a distinct departure from white sand beaches and sparse vegetation, as it is a tree-laden primitive paradise; equestrian, bike, and hiking trails and a picnic area.

ALABAMA

Gulf State Park
Star Route, Box 9
Gulf Shores, Ala. 36542
(205) 968-7544
Largest Gulf Coast park in Alabama, with over 6,000 acres and 2½ miles of white sandy beach; spectacular resort/convention complex; 825-foot fishing pier, off-beach golfing, picnicking, tennis, vacation cottages, freshwater fishing, boating, skiing, swimming.

Little River State Park
Route 2, Box 77
Atmore, Ala. 36502
(205) 862-2511
Fishing and swimming on 25-acre lake, boat rentals, picnicking; primitive campgrounds, vacation cottages.

Florala State Park
Florala, Ala. 36442
(205) 858-6425
On Lake Jackson; picnicking; swimming beach.

Chattahoochee State Park
Star Route, Box 108
Gordon, Ala. 36343
(205) 522-3607
Named for nearby Chattahoochee River; crystal clear lake for fishing; rental boats, picnicking, primitive camping.

TEXAS

Brazos Bend State Park
Route 1, Box 840
Needville, Tex. 77461
(409) 553-3243
Undeveloped beach.

Copano Bay State Park
P.O. Box 39
Fulton, Tex. 78358
(512) 729-8633
Fishing pier.

Galveston Island State Park
Route 1, Box 156A
Galveston, Tex. 77550
(409) 737-1222
Summer drama: "The Lone Star"; camping, picnicking; hiking, nature trails.

Goose Island State Park
Star Route 1, Box 105
Rockport, Tex. 78382
(512) 729-2858
Camping, birdwatching, fishing.

Lake Texana State Park
P.O. Box 666
Edna, Tex. 77957
(512) 782-5718
Fishing, swimming, canoeing, boating, hiking, fishing piers.

Mustang Island State Park
P.O. Box 326
Port Aransas, Tex. 78373
(512) 749-5246
Camping, fishing, nature trails, swimming.

Port Lavaca State Park
114 Linville
Port Lavaca, Tex. 77979
(512) 552-4667
Fishing pier.

Queen Isabella State Park
P.O. Box 2761
South Padre Island, Tex. 78597
(512) 943-9807
Fishing pier.

San Jacinto Battleground
3523 Highway 134
La Porte, Tex. 77571
(713) 479-2431
Battleship *Texas*.

Sea Rim/Sabine Pass Battleground
P.O. Box 1066
Sabine Pass, Tex. 77655
(409) 971-2559
Camping, fishing, crabbing. Four observation blinds for photography; interpretative marsh trails, exhibits, shelling.

Varner-Hogg State Historical Park
P.O. Box 696
West Columbia, Tex. 77486
(409) 345-4656
Museum.

FLORIDA

Big Lagoon State Recreation Area
12301 Gulf Beach Highway
Pensacola, Fla. 32507
(904) 492-1595
Camping, swimming.

Rocky Bayou State Recreation Area
Route 1, Box 597
Niceville, Fla. 32578
(904) 897-3222
Camping, swimming.

Dead Lakes State Recreation Area
P.O. Box 989
Wewahitchka, Fla. 32465
(904) 639-2702
Picnicking, fishing, boating, nature trails; thousands of dead trees in a natural lake formed by blockage of Chipola River.

Grayton Beach State Recreation Area
P.O. Box 25
Santa Rosa Beach, Fla. 32458
(904) 231-4210
Camping, swimming.

Eden Ornamental Garden
P.O. Box 26
Point Washington, Fla. 32454
(904) 231-4214

St. Andrews State Recreation Area
4415 Thomas Drive
Panama City, Fla. 32407
(904) 234-2522
Camping, swimming.

St. Joseph Peninsula State Park
P.O. Box 909
Port St. Joe, Fla. 32456
(904) 227-1327
T. H. Stone Memorial; picnicking, swimming, camping, saltwater fishing, boating, and wilderness hiking; beaches and huge barrier dunes; excellent birding area with 209 species recorded.

Basin Bayou State Recreation Area
P.O. Box 278
Freeport, Fla. 32439
(904) 835-3761
Camping, picnicking, saltwater fishing in bay and bayou.

Constitution Convention State Museum
200 Alden Memorial Way
Port St. Joe, Fla. 32456
(904) 229-8029

John Gorrie State Museum
General Delivery
Apalachicola, Fla.
(904) 653-9347

Fort Gadsden State Historic Site
P.O. Box 457
Sumatra, Fla. 32335
(904) 670-8988

St. George Island State Park
P.O. Box 62
East Point, Fla. 32328
(904) 670-2111
A barrier island with nine miles of undeveloped beaches and dunes; wide variety of migrating birds with 100 species seen on certain days.

Ochlockonee River State Park
P.O. Box 5
Sopchoppy, Fla. 32358
(904) 962-2771
Camping, swimming.

Natural Bridge Battlefield
P.O. Box 27
St. Marks, Fla. 32355
(904) 925-6216
Historic site.

San Marcos De Apalache
P.O. Box 27
St. Marks, Fla. 32355
(904) 925-6216
Historic site.

Forest Capital State Museum
204 Forest Park Drive
Perry, Fla. 32347
(904) 584-3227

Manatee Springs State Park
Route 2, Box 362
Chiefland, Fla. 32626
(904) 493-4288
Crystal clear spring; rare appearance by manatees; picnicking, swimming, boating, fishing, campfire programs, guided nature walks.

Cedar Key State Museum
P.O. Box 538
Cedar Key, Fla. 32625
(904) 543-5350

Crystal River State Archaeological Site
Route 3, Box 610
Crystal River, Fla. 32629
(904) 795-3817

Yulee Sugar Mill Ruins
Route 3, Box 610
Crystal River, Fla. 32629
(904) 795-3817
Historic site.

Caladesi Island State Park
P.O. Box B
Dunedin, Fla. 33528
(813) 443-5903
White sand beach on Gulf side and mangrove swamp on bay side; access only by boat; refuge for many wading and shore birds; nature trails with guided walks; picnicking, boating, swimming, shelling.

Honeymoon Island State Recreation Area
1 Causeway Boulevard
Dunedin, Fla. 33528
(813) 734-4144
Swimming; once joined to Caladesi Island until hurricane of 1921 cut them apart.

Ybor City State Museum
1500 Weedon Island Drive
St. Petersburg, Fla. 33702
(813) 247-6323

Madira Bickel Mound
% Gamble Plantation
Ellenton, Fla. 33532
(813) 722-1017
Archaeological site.

Gamble Plantation
Ellenton, Fla. 33532
(813) 722-1017
Historic site.

Myakka River State Park
Route 1, Box 72
Sarasota, Fla. 33583
(813) 924-1027
Camping.

Koreshan State Historic Site
P.O. Box 7
Estero, Fla. 33928
(813) 992-0311

Lake Manatee State Recreation Area
20007 State Road 64
Bradenton, Fla. 33508
(813) 746-8042
Swimming.

Oscar Scherer State Recreation Area
P.O. Box 398
Osprey, Fla. 33559
(813) 966-3154
Camping, swimming.

Delnor-Wiggins Pass State Recreation Area
11100 Gulf Shore Blvd. North
Naples, Fla. 33940
(813) 597-6196
Swimming.

Collier-Seminole State Park
Marco, Fla. 33937
(813) 394-3397
Vegetation and wildlife representative of Everglades region; interpretative center of exhibits; nature trail, self-guided; camping, boating, canoeing, saltwater fishing; museum.

Fakahatchee Strand State Preserve
P.O. Box 548
Copeland, Fla. 33926
(813) 695-4593
Unusual and rare vegetation and wildlife, including several endangered species; limited facilities with one boardwalk and regular "wet" walks into interior of swamp.

John Pennekamp Coral Reef State Park
P.O. Box 487
Key Largo, Fla. 33037
(305) 451-1202
First underwater state park in U.S.; special feature: nine-foot underwater statue, "Christ of the Deep"; snorkeling, diving, picnicking, camping, swimming, saltwater fishing, and boating.

Lignumvitae Key State Botanical Site
% Long Key State Recreation Area
P.O. Box 776
Long Key, Fla. 33001
(305) 664-4815
Botanical site: rare tropical forest; limited access to key; guided tours.

Indian Key State Historic Site
P.O. Box 776
Long Key, Fla. 33001
(305) 664-4815

Long Key State Recreation Area
P.O. Box 776
Long Key, Fla. 33001
(305) 664-4815
Camping, swimming.

Bahia Honda State Recreation Area
Route 1, Box 782
Big Pine Key, Fla. 33043
(305) 872-2353
Camping, swimming, picnicking, fishing with charter boats and guides, boating, diving, guided walks on nature trail; tropical vegetation and variety of birdlife.

Gulf Coast
National Wildlife Refuges

TEXAS

Santa Ana
Route 1, Box 202A
Alamo, Tex. 78516

Laguna Atascosa
P.O. Box 450
Rio Hondo, Tex. 78583

Aransas
P.O. Box 100
Austwell, Tex. 77950

Attwater Prairie Chicken
P.O. Box 518
Eagle Lake, Tex. 77434

San Bernard
P.O. Box 1088
Angleton, Tex. 77515

Brazoria
P.O. Box 1088
Angleton, Tex. 77515

Anahuac
P.O. Box 278
Anahuac, Tex. 77514

McFaddin
P.O. Box 278
Anahuac, Tex. 77514

Texas Point
P.O. Box 278
Anahuac, Tex. 77514

LOUISIANA

Sabine
MRH 107
Hackberry, La. 70645

Lacassine
Route 1, Box 186
Lake Arthur, La. 70549

Delta-Breton
Venice, La. 70091

MISSISSIPPI

Mississippi Sandhill Crane Complex
2509 Westgate Pkwy.
Gautier, Miss. 39553

FLORIDA

St. Vincent
P.O. Box 447
Apalachicola, Fla. 32320

St. Marks
P.O. Box 68
St. Marks, Fla. 32355

Lower Suwannee
Route 2, Box 44
Homosassa, Fla. 32646

Cedar Keys
Route 2, Box 44
Homosassa, Fla. 32646

Chassahowitzka
Route 2, Box 44
Homosassa, Fla. 32646

Pinellas
P.O. Drawer B
Sanibel, Fla. 33957

Egmont Key
P.O. Drawer B
Sanibel, Fla. 33957

Passage Key
P.O. Drawer B
Sanibel, Fla. 33957

Island Bay
P.O. Drawer B
Sanibel, Fla. 33957

Pine Island
P.O. Drawer B
Sanibel, Fla. 33957

J. N. "Ding" Darling
P.O. Drawer B
Sanibel, Fla. 33957

Matlacha Pass
P.O. Drawer B
Sanibel, Fla. 33957

Great White Heron
P.O. Box 510
Big Pine Key, Fla. 33043

National Key Deer
P.O. Box 510
Big Pine Key, Fla. 33043

Key West
P.O. Box 510
Big Pine Key, Fla. 33043

Notes on Photographs

All photographs were taken with Nikon F, F2, F2A, FE, or F3 35mm cameras. The name of each photograph, along with lens, film, and exposure (when available), is listed below.

pages ii–iii   Horn Island Sunset. 200mm f/4 Nikkor. f/11 @ 1/30. E400. Tripod.

page vi   Golden Marsh. 600mm f/5.6 Nikkor. f/8 @ 1/125. K64. Tripod.

page x   Cameron Parish Beach. 24mm f/2.8 Nikkor. f/11 @ 1/30. K64. Tripod.

page 6   Little Fuzzies. 500mm f/8 Reflex-Nikkor. f/8 @ 1/125. K64. Tripod.

page 8   Oaks and Bromeliads. 16mm f/3.5 Nikkor. f/8 @ 1/30. K64.

page 9   Cow and Calf. 15mm f/2.8 UW Nikkor. f/8 @ 1/60. K64.

page 10   Lichen. 55mm f/3.5 Micro-Nikkor. f/11 @ 1/15. KR. Tripod.

pages 10–11   Choctawhatchee Cypress. 105mm f/2.5 Nikkor. f/8 @ 1/15. K64. Tripod.

page 11   Takeoff. 600mm f/5.6 Nikkor. f/8 @ 1/125. KR. Tripod.

pages 12–13   Rainbow River. 28mm f/3.5 UW Nikkor. f/11 @ 1/60. KR.

page 14   Gator. 200mm f/4 Nikkor. f/8 @ 1/15. KR. Tripod.

page 14   Oaks and Ferns. 24mm f/2.8 Nikkor. f/8 @ 1/15. KR.

page 15   Drying Out. 200mm f/4 Nikkor. f/8 @ 1/125. KR.

page 16   Prickly Pear. 55mm f/3.5 Micro-Nikkor. f/11 @ 1/30. KR. Tripod.

page 17   Yucca. 105mm f/2.5 Nikkor. f/8 @ 1/150. KR. Tripod.

page 17   Spike on the Gulf. 600mm f/5.6 Nikkor. f/5.6 @ 1/250. K64. Tripod.

page 18   Gobblers. 600mm f/5.6 Nikkor. f/5.6 @ 1/250. K64. Tripod.

page 19   Laguna Mockingbird. 200mm f/4 Nikkor. f/8 @ 1/250. K64. Tripod.

page 20   Vulture Roost. 600mm f/5.6 Nikkor. f/5.6 @ 1/30. K64. Tripod.

pages 20–21   Aransas Sunset. 600mm f/5.6 Nikkor. f/8 @ 1/60. K64. Tripod.

page 22   Armadillo. 600mm f/5.6 Nikkor. f/5.6 @ 1/125. K64. Tripod.

page 22   Doe and Broomsedge. 600mm f/5.6 Nikkor. f/5.6 @ 1/60. K64. Tripod.

page 23   Eastern Meadowlark. 600mm f/5.6 Nikkor. f/8 @ 1/60. K64. Tripod.

page 24   Wood Duck Reflection. 600mm f/5.6 Nikkor. f/8 @ 1/60. K64. Tripod.

page 25   Catbird. 600mm f/5.6 Nikkor. f/5.6 @ 1/30. K64. Tripod.

page 25   Viceroy on Hyacinth No. 2. 200mm f/4 Nikkor. f/5.6 @ 1/125. K64.

page 26   Scarlet Tanager. 600mm f/5.6 Nikkor. f/5.6 @ 1/30. K64. Tripod.

page 27   Nesting. 600mm f/5.6 Nikkor. f/8 @ 1/125. K64. Tripod.

page 28   Pilottown. 55mm f/3.5 Micro-Nikkor. f/3.5 @ 1/2000. K64. Helicopter.

page 29   Ghost Ship. 105mm f/2.5 Nikkor. f/5.6 @ 1/125. K64.

pages 30–31   White Ibis. 600mm f/8 Reflex-Nikkor. f/8 @ 1/125. K64. Tripod.

page 32   Beehive. 200mm f/4 Nikkor. f/11 @ 1/30. K64. Tripod.

pages 32–33   Oaks and Moon. 55mm f/3.5 Micro-Nikkor. f/5.6 @ 1/125. K64. Tripod.

page 33   Coon on a Log. 300mm f/4.5 Nikkor. f/11 @ 1/60. K64.

page 34   Mississippi Sunset. 200mm f/4 Nikkor. f/11 @ 1/125. K64.

page 34   Cattails. 105mm f/2.5 Nikkor. f/2.5 @ 1/500. K64.

page 36   Shrimp Boat. 200mm f/4 Nikkor. f/8 @ 1/125. K64.

page 37   Culling Shrimp. 55mm f/3.5 Micro-Nikkor. f/8 @ 1/30. K64.

page 37   Day's Catch. 55mm f/3.5 Micro-Nikkor. f/8 @ 1/30. K64.

pages 38–39   Delta Sunrise. 105mm f/2.5 Nikkor. f/8 @ 1/125. K64. Tripod.

page 40   Tracks. 55mm f/3.5 Micro-Nikkor. f/3.5 @ 1/1000. K64. Plane.

page 41   Least Bittern. 600mm f/5.6 Nikkor. f/5.6 @ 1/250. K64. Tripod.

page 41   Oaks and Hyacinth. 35mm f/3.5 PC Nikkor. f/11 @ 1/60. K64.

page 42   Swimming Coon. 200mm f/4 Nikkor. f/4 @ 1/30. K64.

page 43   Iris. 55mm f/3.5 Micro-Nikkor. f/11 @ 1/8. K64. Tripod.

page 44   Long Legs. 600mm f/5.6 Nikkor. f/5.6 @ 1/60. K64. Tripod.

pages 44–45   Marsh Sunrise. 24mm f/2.8 Nikkor. f/8 @ 1/25. K64. Tripod.

page 45   Swamp Rabbit. 500mm f/8 Reflex Nikkor. f/8 @ 1/60. E200. Tripod.

page 46   Kingbird's Nest. 200mm f/4 Nikkor. f/5.6 @ 1/60. K64.

page 47   Bucket of Crabs. 55mm f/3.5 Micro-Nikkor. f/11 @ 1/15. K64. Tripod.

page 47   Pods. 55mm f/3.5 Micro-Nikkor. f/11 @ 1/30. K64. Tripod.

page 48   White Flight. 200mm f/4 Nikkor. f/4 @ 1/500. K64. Helicopter.

page 48   Willets. 600mm f/5.6 Nikkor. f/5.6 @ 1/60. K64. Tripod.

page 49   Gator in Duckweed. 105mm f/2.5 Nikkor. f/8 @ 1/30. K64.

page 50   Hyacinth. 105mm f/2.5 Nikkor. f/11 @ 1/60. K64. Fill flash.

pages 50–51   Marsh Pond. 24mm f/2.8 Nikkor. f/11 @ 1/125. K64.

page 52   Roseate. 600mm f/5.6 Nikkor. f/5.6 @ 1/60. K64. Tripod.

page 53   Tricolored Heron. 600mm f/5.6 Nikkor. f/5.6 @ 1/125. K64. Tripod.

page 54   Cormorant. 600mm f/5.6 Nikkor. f/8 @ 1/60. K64. Tripod.

page 54   Softshell Turtle. 200mm f/4 Nikkor. f/4 @ 1/30. K64.

page 55   Coot Parade. 600mm f/5.6 Nikkor. f/8 @ 1/60. K64. Tripod.

pages 56–57   Coots in Fog. 200mm f/4 Nikkor. f/4 @ 1/250. K64. Tripod.

page 58   Frog's not Home. 105mm f/2.5 Nikkor. f/11 @ 1/15. K64. Tripod.

page 58   Needlerush. 105mm f/2.5 Nikkor. f/4 @ 1/60. K64.

page 59   Salt-marsh Pink. 55mm f/3.5 Micro-Nikkor. f/16 @ 1/30. K64. Tripod.

page 60   Railroad Vine. 35mm f/3.5 PC Nikkor. f/8 @ 1/25. K64.

pages 60–61   Tropical Sunset. 600mm f/5.6 Nikkor. f/8 @ 1/250. K64. Tripod.

page 61   Nutria. 200mm f/4 Nikkor. f/4 @ 1/250. E260.

pages 62–63   Louisiana Marsh. 55mm f/3.5 Micro-Nikkor. f/3.5 @ 1/2000. E200. Plane.

page 64   Black Beauty. 600mm f/5.6 Nikkor. f/8 @ 1/60. K64. Tripod.

page 65   Porpoise. 200mm f/4 Nikkor. f/4 @ 1/250. K64.

Custom prints of all photographs used in this book are available for purchase. A limited quantity are printed in sizes 16 × 20 and 11 × 14. For information contact: The Lockwood Gallery
P.O. Box 14876
Baton Rouge, Louisiana 70898

Index